CONTENTS

© Chancerel Publishers 1981

First published in this edition 1981 by
Octopus Books Limited
59, Grosvenor Street,
London W1.

Produced by Chancerel Publishers Limited,
40, Tavistock Street,
London WC2E 7PB.

ISBN 0 7064 1612 0

Printed in Hong Kong

Origination by Reprosharp, London EC1
and La Comolito, Milan.

Photographs
Tencate (Windsurfer) pages 6, 12, 22, 34, 40, 46.
Alastair Black 56, 66.

The publishers would like to acknowledge the
assistance of the London Windsurfing School in
the preparation of this book.

Additional illustrations by Shirley Hooper

LET'S GO
WINDSURFING

Text by Graeme Fuller
Edited by Jim Miles
Illustrations by René Deynis

WINDSURFING—THE SPORT

When you have experienced the sensation of the
sea speeding under your sailboard as it leaps over the waves
you will realize why windsurfing is the ultimate
in free rides and the fastest growing water sport.

This book is aimed to tempt, guide and encourage you as a mildly interested individual into becoming a devotee of one of the most interesting and diverse of water-bound recreations – sailboarding. No matter how long you spend at it, you will never be bored nor find a limit to how much you can learn from being at one with the wind and waves. So read on and discover the ups and downs, for there will be many – sailboarding is not the easiest of sports to master, but then truly rewarding pursuits seldom are.

This book is intended to introduce you to the sport, show you how it all started and how it is developing. It will explain how the sailboard works and how you can sail it safely. Hopefully you will progress to the spectacular and exhilarating freestyle techniques described towards the end of the book. The sport is called windsurfing, board sailing or sailboarding. In this book we refer to it as windsurfing – the accepted form for the whole sport. Where Windsurfer appears with a capital W this refers to the patented craft. Technical terms are shown in bold letters and appear in the glossary on page 76.

A board sailor experiencing the sensations of wind and waves on a Windsurfer.

The birth of the sport

The two men responsible for the sport as we know it today are both Americans from Southern California, Jim Drake and Hoyle Schweitzer. Though this is a part of the world from which all kinds of sports and pastimes come, Drake and Schweitzer developed something destined to become far more than just a passing craze. Drake's full time job was as an aeronautical designer and his hobby was sailing. His friend Schweitzer was a perceptive businessman and keen surfer. Their numerous discussions together produced the idea of a sailing surfboard.

Drake had been vaguely considering some such system for five years or so and his early ideas centred around a craft powered and steered by a flying kite. The problem was how to steer the surfboard and though a foot-operated rudder was considered the idea did not work in practice. Two vital facts were known: firstly, any sailing craft can be steered by the set of the sails alone without using a rudder and secondly, a surfboard is steered by body action. The two men strove to make use of these facts.

Drake came up with the idea of a moveable mast while driving home from a business trip. He went ahead and produced the moveable mast foot in two forms. One allowed the mast to tip forwards and backwards only, while the other allowed it to fall in any direction by using a **universal joint** (see page 15). The first system proved to be impractical and the second system had its problems. It was difficult to raise the sail and, once under way, the tail of the board went from side to side or 'fishtailed'. These problems were overcome by attaching a rope to the boom to raise the sail from the water and by adding a tailfin or **skeg** under the board to cure the fishtail effect. The boom that Drake used was called the **wish-**

bone because of its shape and though it was not a new idea this was certainly a new application. In the meantime Schweitzer had been busy producing a large surfboard designed to carry the **rig** of mast and sail.

Craft of several shapes and sizes were constructed using the revolutionary 'free sail system'

A Windsurfer in action – 150,000 boards of this design were made. The universal joint allows the mast to tilt.

as it was called, and these prototypes were sailed by Schweitzer and his friends. It was not long before casual enquiries from passers-by turned into commercial propositions so the business-minded Schweitzer decided to patent the idea.

Schweitzer's first production boards were called SK-8s (Skates) and, like surfboards, were made from hand laid fibreglass and were therefore very expensive. In his search for a material that would be cheaper yet more lasting than fibreglass, Schweitzer came up with polyethylene which was then being successfully used in the manufacture of the Frisbee. This was such a totally new use of the material that Dupont, the suppliers of polyethylene, published an article that was to give the brainchild of Drake and Schweitzer worldwide fame. The Windsurfer had been born.

As a result of the publicity that Dupont had given to the Windsurfer a deluge of orders came in from Europe particularly Germany. The International Windsurfing Schools (IWS) were started up on the continent using a land based simulator which allowed the sport to be taught 'dry'. A further result was that a major Dutch textile company called Tencate became interested in the Windsurfer and took out a licence to produce it in Holland. This combined with the IWS schooling system meant that sailboarding was all set to take off in a big way.

The chilly European climate and the relative shortage of water on which to sail did not discourage interest. Boards began selling in their thousands with European sales soon outstripping American sales.

Tencate began production of the Windsurfer in 1973 and were soon followed by other companies making cheaper, but inferior, glassfibre copies. Between 1973 and 1978 an estimated 150,000 boards were sold on the continent in an atmosphere of fierce rivalry between the various manufacturers. Those companies who had been licensed by Schweitzer to produce Windsurfers were particularly upset by the large number of unlicensed companies and lengthy legal battles took place. Those who did not have a licence did have an ace up their sleeves however. His name was Newman Darby.

In 1965 Newman Derby, yet another American, published an article in the magazine Popular Science. It had this wordy title: 'Sailboarding: An Exciting New Water Sport for High-speed Water Fun.' It went on to claim that this was '. . . a sport so new that fewer than ten people have yet mastered it.' Darby's sailboard was designed to be sailed with his back to the rig.

Although the idea did not catch on at the time it did provide hope for those trying to challenge Schweitzer's patent and manufacture cheaper boards.

The Windsurfer

Companies situated around the world soon gave the Windsurfer an international following and as it was such good fun to race it was possible to establish a class association on a worldwide basis. This was designed to link all Windsurfer owners and to provide guidelines for competitions at national and international levels.

Since the Windsurfer has sold so well and so widely it has been possible to organize competitions in which everyone has to use the same make of board without the use of any modifications or extras. This means that everyone taking part stands to succeed or fail simply by their own ability.

The International Windsurfer Class Association (IWCA) has recently been recognized by the International Yacht Racing Union (IYRU) and this has given the sport an additional air of respectability. The second boost to the sport came when the Olympic committee met at the Moscow Olympics and accepted Boardsailing or Windsurfing as an Olympic class to be contested at the 1984 Olympics.

For racing purposes the Windsurfer board does have a few disadvantages which have become apparent over the years. The board is not sufficiently' bouyant to support a really heavy person which does give an edge to lightweight

A sailboard is rudderless and is steered by body action. In this unique form of sailing the mast is supported by the board sailor, not stays.

9

sailors. This is reflected in the fact that the racing is conducted in four weight divisions plus a ladies division. Also the fibreglass mast is very flexible and in strong winds can bend too much. This destroys the sail shape and makes the board extremely difficult to handle. Another drawback is that the teak wishbone boom though robust, is also very heavy and more difficult to use than the lighter and more common aluminium boom.

The Windglider

The Windglider is made under licence in Germany where it has sold very well and taken over

from the Windsurfer as the brand leader. It has more bouyancy than the Windsurfer and is therefore easier to sail for the heavier person. This, combined with an aluminium boom and larger sail area, makes the Windglider faster than the Windsurfer.

The superior speed of the Windglider was confirmed when a Dutchman, Dirk Thijs, went to the Weymouth Sailing Speed Trials in 1977 and astounded the sailing world by breaking the world speed record for craft with under 10m² (11 sq. yds) of sail area. Using a special lightweight Windglider, he set a speed of 19.01 knots which

did wonders for the sales of the craft.

It now has the second largest sales worldwide and so a similar class association to that of the Windsurfer has been formed which also is recognized by the IYRU.

With all this going on interest in sailboards has greatly increased. And the sailing world in general now looks upon the sport respectfully and seriously. The future for sailboarding as a leisure pursuit or serious sailing sport has never looked better.

More and more people are taking up sailboard. And now that it is an Olympic sport, it will receive even more public attention.

An Open Class regatta. It soon became popular to race sailboards and manufacturers were quick to make faster boards with bigger sails.

11

THE SAILBOARD

The standard sailboard has seven basic parts.
Although refinements and improvements are being
added to sailboards all the time, few major changes
have been made to the Windsurfer as designed by
Jim Drake and Hoyle Schweitzer in 1969.

There are three main types of modern sailboard.
The most common has a rounded nose and tail.
It is suitable for beginners and all-purpose use
by experienced sailors. Then there is the high
performance board, which is excellent for
regatta sailing, with its extra speed upwind. The
third type of board is designed for use in waves
and surf. This highly specialized kind of board is
flat with straight sides and a large **bow scoop**, or
rocker, twin skegs and sometimes **footstraps**.

One feature all these boards share is the universal joint, coupling the mast and the hull.

The standard board

Today all sailboards are made in a mould, using
glassfibre, polyethylene or a type of hard plastic
called ABS. Generally the board is filled with
expanded polyethelene foam, which makes it
totally unsinkable. Even if it is broken in half,
each part should have enough bouyancy to keep
a man afloat.

A good board looks sleek. It has no sharp

*The Tencate TC39 an advanced
design of sailboard, with good upwind
performance.*

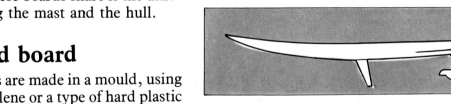

*A standard-type board such as a Windsurfer, is flat
with rounded edges and is easy to sail.*

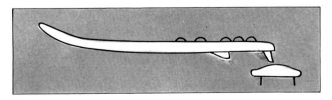

*A wave jumping board has an upswept nose, twin
skegs, a smaller daggerboard and footstraps.*

*A regatta board has a deep, rounded hull shape like
a sailing dinghy and a retractable daggerboard.*

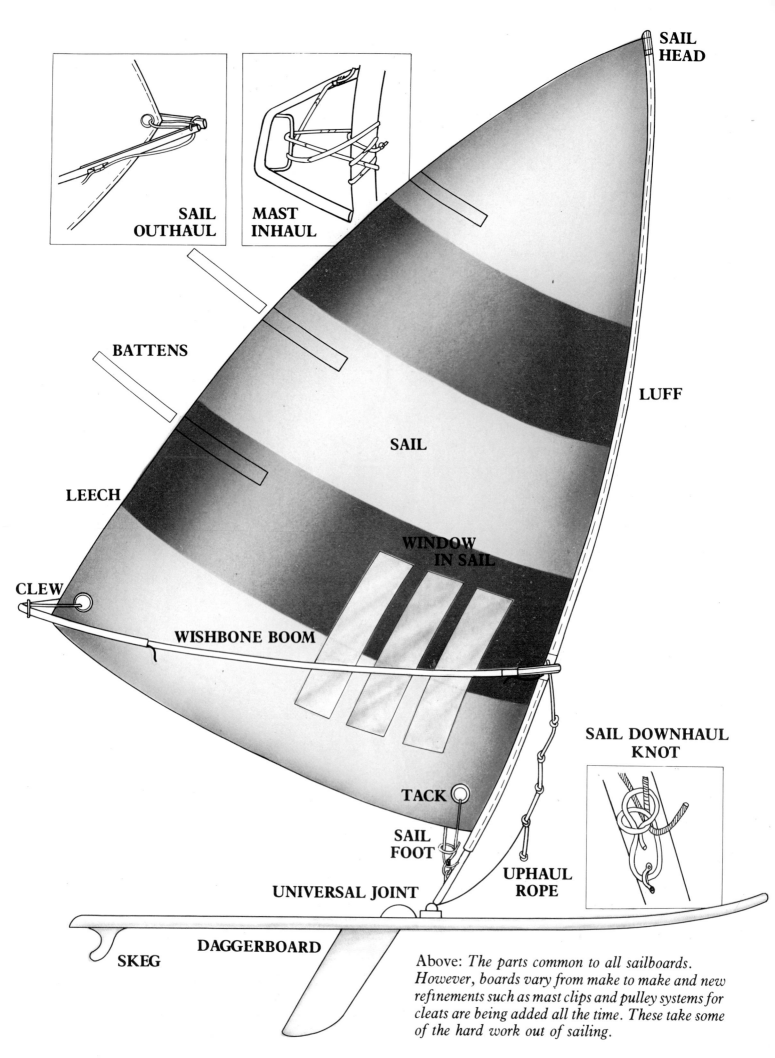

SAIL
OUTHAUL

MAST
INHAUL

SAIL
HEAD

BATTENS

LUFF

SAIL

LEECH

WINDOW
IN SAIL

CLEW

WISHBONE BOOM

SAIL DOWNHAUL
KNOT

TACK

SAIL
FOOT

UPHAUL
ROPE

UNIVERSAL JOINT

SKEG

DAGGERBOARD

Above: *The parts common to all sailboards. However, boards vary from make to make and new refinements such as mast clips and pulley systems for cleats are being added all the time. These take some of the hard work out of sailing.*

edges which might cause injury in an accident. Yet it needs to be rugged and durably built. Polyethylene and ABS boards have the advantage in this respect.

All-round boards tend to be rounded at the stern and bows, with soft **chines** – the edges of the board.

All boards need a good non-slip surface, to help the sailor grip with his feet. In the middle of the board there is a well, which houses the **daggerboard**, or **centre board**. This provides all-important stability and lateral resistance (see page 24), which enables the craft to move upwind. Finally on the rear underside of the board there is another vital feature, the skeg, or tail fin, which gives directional stability.

Most general purpose boards on the market are about 3.5m (12ft) long, 60-70cm (24-27ins) wide and weigh 20-27kg (45-60lbs), not including the mast and sail.

The rig The rig consists of the mast, the sail and the wishbone boom which are connected to the board by the universal joint. All the parts are held together with ropes and cleats, plastic couplings and screws, varying from make to make.

Rigging the sailboard The first step in rigging the board is to slide the mast into the sleeve of the sail. One third of the way up the sail there is a cutaway section. This makes it possible to lash the leading edge of the boom to the mast. This lashing must be very tight – all the sailboard's control depends on this connection.

At this point the universal joint is slotted into the mast and tied to the foot of the sail. This fixing can be adjusted later, according to the strength of the wind and the sailing conditions.

The sail is normally supplied with battens. These have to be slipped into the pockets in the sail, before pulling it firmly out to the end of the boom. Depending on the make of the board, the sail is tied directly to the end of the boom, or cleated to the boom with a rope and pulley system.

All that now remains to be done is to attach the uphaul rope to the boom, the elastic shock cord to the universal joint and the board is ready to sail – simplicity itself.

The universal joint There are dozens of types of universal joint. But they all fit into one of two categories. Firstly, there is the mechanical type and secondly, the flexible variety, made of solid rubber, or nylon composite.

The most important thing to check is the way in which the universal joint fits the board. It must plug into the hull firmly enough to hold while sailing. But it must also pull out in an emergency. It is all too easy to trap your foot between the mast and the board, while you are under the sail, in the water. In a case like this you need to be able to disentangle yourself fast.

Inspect your universal joint carefully before you go out sailing – every time. If you see any signs of wear or damage, do not hesitate to replace it. And after you have been sailing make sure you remove any grit or sand that may have become caught in it.

The mast As with universal joints, there are two basic types of mast. One is made of glassfibre and the other of aluminium. Glassfibre is generally better for all-purpose boards. Aluminium

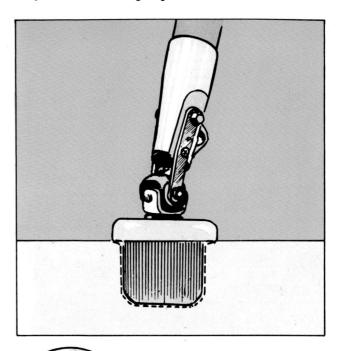

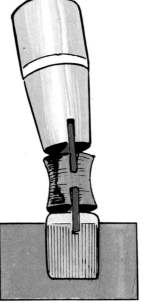

Mechanical universal joints (above) are long lasting, but cost more. They have the disadvantage of being hard and painful if accidentally kicked with a bare tow. On the other hand the flexible universals (left) are sometimes cheap and very shoddy. Inspect them carefully before you buy. The mast foot should fit firmly into the board.

Different sails are designed for different conditions. This all-weather sail is being used in breaking surf.

is preferred by racing enthusiasts because it is more rigid. This lack of flexibility is good for speed but it is most easily dented, bent and scratched.

Glassfibre masts are made from layers of resin and glassfibre, wound together to produce a tapered shape. The result is a mast that bends more at the top than the bottom, which in turn produces the ideal sail shape.

The sail Before discussing the sail, it will help to know a few technical terms. The top of the sail is known as the **head**. The bottom edge is the

foot. The eyelet at the bottom corner is the **tack**. The **clew** is the eyelet used to secure the sail to the outer limit of the boom. The **outhaul rope** keeps the sail tight. The leading edge of the sail is the **luff**. The **luff sleeve** is the part of the sail that slides over the mast. The trailing edge of the sail, into which the battens are fitted, is called the **leech**.

Most boards come equipped with a standard sail usually about 5.4m²-6.5m² (59 sq ft) in size. This is a colourful triangle made of synthetic rot-proof panels, with large, clear windows set into it. Good visibility is essential to the board-sailor, so the windows are at head height.

Although the sailcloth is very resilient, it has to withstand being soaked in seawater repeatedly, having bodies thrown into it, being left screwed up on the beach and being creased into a sail bag. All this is inevitable, but it will still pay you to look after your sail. Dry it after use if possible. Always wrap it around the mast, disconnecting the boom to do so, especially if it is in storage for a long period.

If you wish to fold up your sail, do so along the panel seams. Then make it into the largest roll you can store conveniently.

When you come to use the sail again, examine carefully the clew, the tack and head for wear. The two most common problems with the sail are the clew pulling out and the mast shooting through the head. Either or both can leave you with a long paddle back to shore or an embarrassing rescue.

If battens are supplied, make sure you use them. A sail will deteriorate quickly it is used without battens, as the leech will flap. Never fold the sail with the battens in place.

Remember, the sail is your power source, your engine. As with all engines, it needs care and attention if it is to provide you with long service. Neglect invariably leads to a break-down.

Types of sail Apart from the standard sail, there are several other shapes and sizes available to the board sailor. These range from large, light weather sails, to the 6m² (65sq ft) high performance, regatta sails.

The more extreme the conditions, the smaller the sail you should use. The sizes, in decreasing order, are the **marginal,** the **all-weather,** and the **storm sail,** the smallest of all. These three types are not usually provided with battens, so you must supply them yourself. They are only intended for use in wind strengths of force four and above.

Booms A sailboard boom is basically a powerful lever, which you use to steer the sailboard and maintain your balance. At one time or another you will have to hold it from both sides. It is therefore designed to run right round the sail, using either two semi-circular sections, or in some cases, two parallel bars, joined at the ends by U-sections.

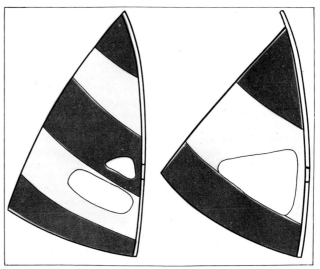

Left: *Standard sail as supplied with most sailboards.*
Right: *Marginal sail for use in surf and waves.*

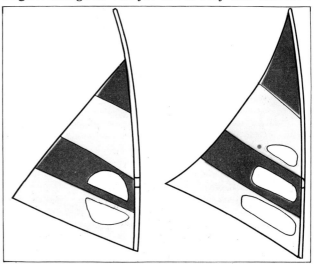

Left: *Storm sail for use in very high winds.*
Right: *All-weather sail.* Below: *regatta sail.*

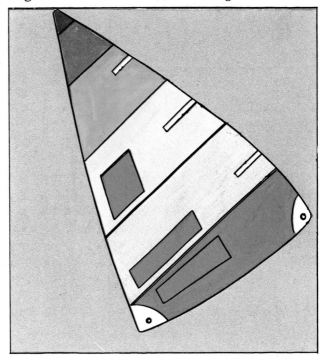

The wishbone boom originally supplied with the Windsurfer is made of laminated teak and connected at one end by a W strip, shaped like the letter. This is covered with a padded boom bumper to protect both the sailor and the board from damage on impact.

Aluminium booms though lighter and cheaper than teak booms, do have drawbacks. They are hollow and riveted in places. If they are badly made water can seep in through the rivet holes and fill the boom making it heavy and difficult to pull up. Be careful not to put too much strain on an aluminium boom in heavy surf conditions. It can bend, leaving a permanent kink.

Some booms are taped in red and green, for port and starboard, a useful feature for beginners.

At the front end of the boom there is a cleat for the **mast inhaul** line. And at the rear of it there is another for the **sail outhaul**. The uphaul rope is

The wishbone boom provides an experienced board sailor with acceleration braking and steering.

simply tied to the W strip on the front end of the boom so that you can use it to pull the boom clear of the water. The uphaul is also knotted at various intervals along its length, so that your hands do not slip when you are pulling up the rig. The first knot should be approximately one hand's breadth from the boom and the last at the end of the rope.

Care of the boom The boom is your sole means of steering, acceleration and braking – the means of controlling the board. It is in your hands all the time you are sailing, so it is vital that it is comfortable, strong and easily manouverable.

Make sure that it is well protected at the front, with a good bumper. If not it will almost certainly damage your board, and it may damage you as

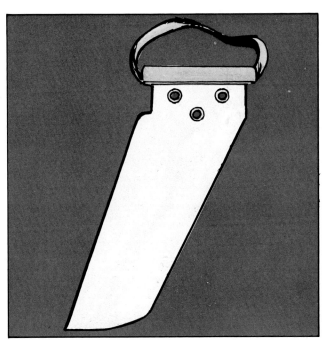

A standard daggerboard. When sailing downwind it can be pulled out by the strap and put over an arm.

well, if it falls on your head – a distinct possibility early on in your sailing career.

Always check that in the event of damage while you are sailing, it is possible to lash the boom to the mast temporarily. A weekend's sailing can be ruined by a broken clip, or if the break occurs at sea, the situation could be far more serious.

Twin clam cleats and pulley systems make sail tensioning and adjustments easier, especially under way, using two bowline loops on either end of the outhaul rope.

A good boom requires little or no attention and should give long and trouble-free service. If it is teak it may need rubbing down and treating with

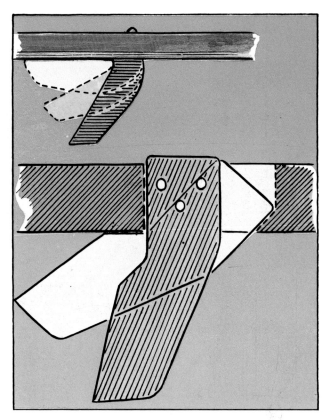

A swivel daggerboard can be kicked back while underway to allow the board to travel faster.

teak oil – never with varnish, which ruins the grip. On aluminium booms the grip tape or rubber can be damaged quite easily. This can be retaped.

The daggerboard The daggerboard provides stability and lateral resistance. Like the keel of a boat, it stops the board slipping sideways through the water. The daggerboard is shaped to produce as little resistance as possible to forward motion,

A storm daggerboard is small and fixed. It prevents the hydrofoil effect caused by normal daggerboards.

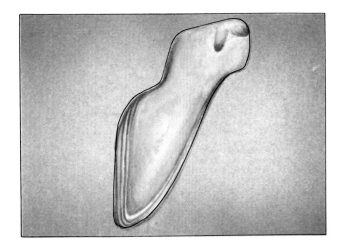

while giving lift to assist upwind performance. This is a complex subject that will be explained later.

Daggerboards are made of wood or plastic or a composite material. They are held in a case in the centre of the board, so that they project below it under the water.

Originally daggerboards were either kept in position while sailing or removed altogether. For high speed sailing they could be withdrawn and hung over one arm (see page 47). Recent advances in design have produced the swivel daggerboard

Acutec were the first firm to produce a radical board design with their Hi Fly.

and some racing boards even have a fully retractable daggerboard.

Vario, or swivel daggerboards can be set in different positions. Another advantage they have is that if you hit an underwater obstacle, or run up the beach, you do not necessarily damage your board.

A useful extra to the boardsailor's equipment

list is a storm daggerboard. This is much smaller and swept further aft than the normal daggerboard.

The other reason to have a smaller or swept back daggerboard is because larger daggerboards tend to act like a hydro-foil at high speed, tilting the sailboard onto its side – and its passenger into the water!

Care of daggerboards Wooden daggerboards should be kept smooth with wet-and-dry paper. They need to be varnished frequently to protect the wood, which can become soft and waterlogged after repeated scratching on rocks and sand.

Plastic and composite daggerboards are generally more durable from this point of view, but they are likely to warp and bend if left lying around in the sun, especially if supporting the weight of the sailboard. If damaged they are usually easily repaired with a glassfibre repair kit.

Skegs Skegs are a subject of constant discussion among expert surfers and boardsailors. For such a small part of the outfit their importance seems over-rated. But try sailing a board in winds over force four without one and you'll soon realize the importance of that little piece of plastic.

As with all other parts of the sailboard, skegs vary from board to board in fixtures and sizes. The skeg provides directional stability, and assists in the steering actions required to manoeuvre the craft. Its importance increases with the windstrength – so don't trim it down, whatever other board sailors might say.

Skegs are generally made of plastic. Some are designed to crack on severe impact, rather than damaging the board. They need little or no attention, save making sure they are still there before a trip.

Design advances

The equipment described so far could be virtually any of the standard boards. Most of them were based on the original Windsurfer, Windglider and Mistral models. But now design developments that have resulted from competition among manufacturers and competition among sailboard enthusiasts are filtering through to standard boards.

When it was realized in Europe how much fun was to be had in racing Windsurfers, new ideas were incorporated into board design. The new sailboards were built specially, either for racing, or for high performance in waves and surf.

As the sport began to boom, organizations were formed and rules drawn up restricting the measurements of boards and sail areas. Developments were therefore restricted to hull design.

The Windglider was the first board after the Windsurfer to make any great impact on the market. It was more bouyant, longer, lighter and consequently faster than the Windsurfer.

Tencate, the European manufacturers of the Windsurfer, soon responded with their new hull, called the TC 39. This had a long V-shaped hull, which drastically improved its upwind performance.

Shortly after this, the German firm Acutec produced a revolutionary hull shape made in polyethylene, which was very fast as well as being attractive in appearance. Its speed was largely due to its special hull shape, a semi-displacement design, more like a sailing dinghy than a surf board.

However, as the boards became more and more extreme in shape, they also became more difficult to sail. Boards like the Windglider Mach 1, Tornado, and Alpha Pro have many of the characteristics of miniature racing dinghies. There are only a handful of people in the whole of Europe capable of sailing them without falling in constantly.

These sailboards are all raced in the so-called Open Class where the stakes are high. Regatta sailboards have full size 6m² (65 sq ft) sails, booms with a pulley system for adjusting the sail and in some cases a kicking strap for adjusting sail foot and leech tension.

The spin-off advantages for less ambitious and less well off sailboarders appeared rapidly. Adjustable daggerboards, which can be swivelled while you are underway, with the foot or the hand, are now common. Sails are now often fitted with tapered racing battens to keep them in the best shape for sailing. Fast boards are now easier to handle. They are built of better materials and they have better rigs. They are more brightly coloured and, most important of all, they have extra features such as safety leashes already attached.

LEARNING TO WINDSURF

Now you are familiar with the sailboard and its parts,
the next step is to master the basic principles of
sailing it. This will take determination and practice, but it
will be well worth it in the end.

As you try and raise the sail and fall in backwards for yet another unplanned ducking it may occur to you that windsurfing and you are not meant for each other. Experienced board sailors sweep past with a nonchalant wave and a knowing look. (You remind them of how they were when they first started.) Determined to become as good as them you scramble back onto your board – windsurfing is like that. Professional instruction can make it much easier and this chapter is loosely based on the sequence of events that takes place when you enrol with a commercial windsurfing school.

Sailing theory

If you hoist a flag in wind there are no prizes for guessing in which direction it will flutter. Similarly, if you drop a feather – you would not expect to see it move in the opposite direction to the wind (move **upwind**). How then is it possible for yachts and sailing craft to sail in all directions of the compass regardless of the wind direction?

To start with it is not absolutely true to say that a sailcraft can move in any direction. It achieves its upwind performance, as experienced sailors know, by **tacking** whilst sailing at an angle of approximately 45 degrees to the **true**

A crowd of Windsurfers jostle for position at the start of a regatta.

wind direction (the wind blowing at the time). But even this may well seem a contradiction in terms since it still means that craft can move against the wind.

Without being too technical, movement is achieved by the difference in pressure created when the airstream flows over the curvature of the sail. As a sail is **sheeted in** the airflow is divided into two streams: one flows over the windward side and the other the leeward side. Because of the sail curvature or camber, the windward airstream is compressed, creating the sail curve, whilst the leeward airstream has to travel further and therefore faster. This causes a difference in pressure between the two sides of the sail. There is less pressure on the leeward side so air attempts to correct the difference by flowing to this low pressure area. The sail is pulled towards the leeward direction by suction, and this provides the propulsion.

Two other important factors common to all sailing craft are the keel (or daggerboard in the case of a sailboard), and the **apparent wind** created by the craft's movement through the water.

Setting a sail alone would result simply in the craft being pushed downwind, but introduce a form of lateral resistance (see page 24) against the water to prevent movement to leeward, and the drive can be converted into forward movement.

In absolutely still air, the movement of an object in any direction, creates an equal and opposite wind which you can feel when riding a bicycle, say. This wind combines with the true wind that exists to form the apparent wind, and it is this that actually drives the board or boat through the water.

The faster a board travels the more apparent wind is created. This is why it is possible for some craft to actually sail faster than the wind.

Points of sailing

The illustration on page 25 shows the various directions in which a sailboard can travel. It is possible to move upwind in tacks, which is also known as **beating** or sailing **close-hauled**. When sailing **dead before the wind** or **running** the wind is directly behind. A **beam reach** is sailing at 90 degrees to the wind, and a **broad reach** is sailing between a beam reach and running.

How can a craft without a rudder be sailed in these various directions? This takes us back to theory again. The sailboard sail has a **centre of**

A sailboard's movement through the water and the true wind combine to form the 'apparent wind'.

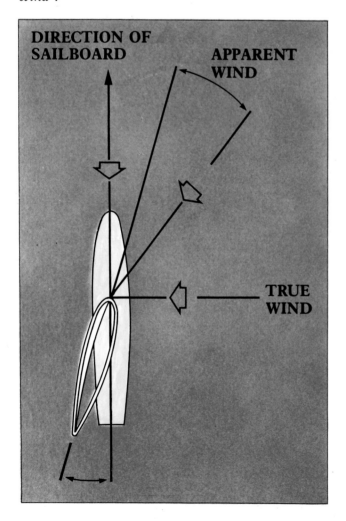

DIRECTION OF
SAILBOARD

APPARENT
WIND

TRUE
WIND

effort, i.e. an imaginery centre of all the wind power acting upon the sail. This point does not occur at the dead centre of the sail dimensionally, but depends on the angle of attack of the wind forces acting upon it. It can move around in the general area indicated on the illustration on page 26.

The daggerboard, as already explained, offers lateral resistance to the water. This too has a single point and it is called the **central point of lateral resistance**. When the sail is raked forward its centre of effort moves ahead of the central point of lateral resistance and causes the board to run away from the wind or **bear off**. If the action is reversed and the sail is raked aft, the stern of the board will fall away causing the board to head up into the wind or **luff**. It is from this movement that a tack usually follows. The board is brought head to wind, the board sailor moves around the mast and bears off in the opposite direction. With these two simple movements all points of sailing can be achieved.

After a lot of practice you will find these routines easy to do, but first you have to learn how to balance on the board, pull up the rig from the water, sheet in and actually get moving.

Into the water

Suitably kitted in your wetsuit and sailing shoes you are now ready for the big splash. On the water board sailors are zipping about and you cannot wait to join them. You shove your board onto the water, eventually manage to make a wobbly stand, heave on the uphaul to tug the rig clear of the water and end up in the water yourself. Welcome to windsurfing!

Several falls later and you are back on the shore shivering. It is time to go through that simulator again.

The land-based simulator If you should attend a commercial windsurfing school, one of the most valuable assets you will encounter is the land-based windsurfing simulator. This is either a wooden board, or a sawn-off sailboard mounted on a spring swivel system, suitably dampened to give the impression of being on the water. On this mechanism an instructor can easily demonstrate the procedures for lifting the rig, setting the sail, steering the board and so on.

The tethered board The techniques taught on the simulator are now put into practice on a board on the water which will be tethered to prevent beginners drifting off over the horizon.

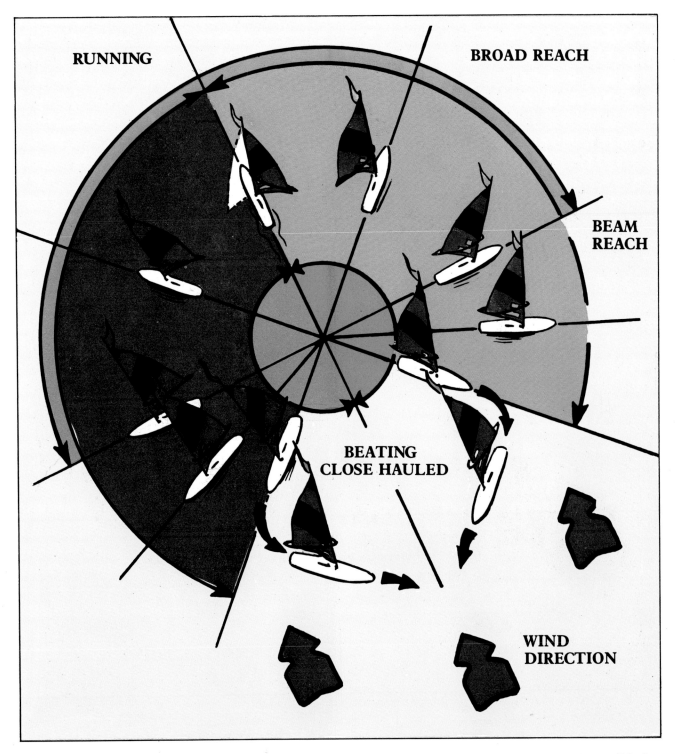

RUNNING

BROAD REACH

BEAM REACH

BEATING CLOSE HAULED

WIND DIRECTION

The board will already have been launched and tied up. So you will have to swim out to the board and climb on. Immediately you will notice how unstable the craft can be. It is best to stay low at first until you have become used to the wobbles. Kneel on or around the daggerboard case until you feel steady and then get up, using the uphaul rope as a support if necessary.

Raising the sail The board should be at right angles to the wind with the sail lying on the downwind side. Attempt to lift the rig clear by placing your feet on either side of the mast foot,

The points of sailing: The directions it is possible for a sailcraft to sail in with any given wind are shown above. The yellow sector is unobtainable by any direct means.

spread evenly and about 45cm (18 ins) apart.

If you snatch or strain to rip the rig clear, it will not come. To begin with it is best to hold the uphaul and lean back against it, and rocking until the mast tip clears the water. Now begin to apply some effort, bending your legs and crouching, then straightening your legs and holding with both hands begin to lift. (Do not

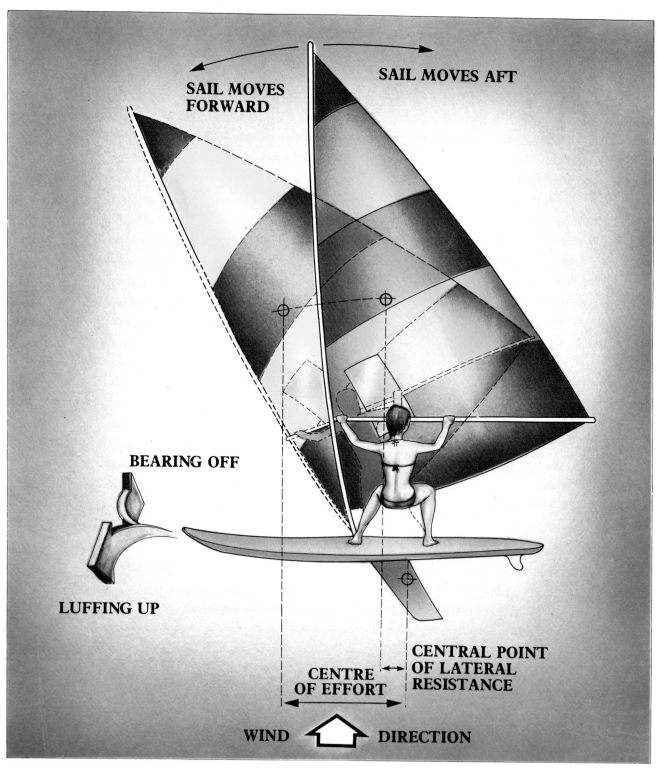

SAIL MOVES FORWARD

SAIL MOVES AFT

BEARING OFF

LUFFING UP

CENTRE OF EFFORT

CENTRAL POINT OF LATERAL RESISTANCE

WIND DIRECTION

use your back muscles.) Slowly and surely the rig will rise clear. Remember it is full of water, and is more than twice its normal weight. As it comes up water drains away quite quickly and you are suddenly left with very little weight to counterbalance your own weight. This rapidly leads to a dip or two until you have mastered the technique of balancing on the board with the sail flapping.

Having raised the rig the next step is to ascertain which is going to be your mast hand and which the sheet hand. The mast hand holds the

A sailboard is steered by raking the sail forward – to bear away from the wind and aft, to luff up into the wind. Two other important factors are the 'centre of effort' in the sail and the 'centre of lateral resistance' in the daggerboard.

boom near to the mast and acts like a pivot whilst the sheet hand draws in the sail and controls your speed.

The board at this point should be at right angles to the wind, with the sail flapping dead downwind. During your earlier attempts at pul-

Raising the sail
Left: *Crouch on the board to get your balance using the uphaul to steady yourself.*
Right: *With the uphaul in your hand, stand up and drag the sail into the downwind position.*
Bottom left: *Bend your knees slowly straighten and raise the mast tip clear of the water.*
Bottom right: *As the rig comes clear it becomes lighter as water drains off the sail. Practise balancing with the rig in the mast abeam position.*

ling up the rig, you may have fallen in to windward dragging the rig in with you. This is the curse of all beginners and means dragging the sail back to the downwind side and starting all over again, but whatever you do, do not get into the habit of prematurely letting go to make sure the rig falls downwind.

Getting underway The board is at last pointing in the direction you wish to go (right angles to the wind). You must now release the uphaul rope with your mast hand, which is the hand nearest to the front of the board, cross it over the hand still holding the uphaul and place it onto the boom adjacent to the mast.

With the bottom of the sail at right angles to the board you must now rake the rig forward and across your body to windward twisting your shoulders as you go. Take the rig across the board until the lower part of the mast nearly touches your shin. The sail will continue to flap in the breeze until you transfer the hand still holding the rope (the sheet hand) to the boom about 60cm (2 ft) from the other hand. Now slowly **sheet in** (pull the rig in using the mast hand as a pivot). Do not let the mast hand move from its position until you are under way. This should happen the moment the sail fills as you sheet in.

As the sail fills you will feel the rig's power,

27

trying to pull you into the water. A common way to prevent this is the urge to stick out the bottom to counter the effect. Although this is totally wrong, beginners always seem to do it at first, and only practice will prevent it. The problem is that by doing it you get a momentary respite, but your own centre of gravity is moved in the wrong direction making it even easier for the next puff of wind to drag you in. You are then unable to perform the correct recovery procedure, which is to let go of the sheet hand, bring the mast hand back to its correct position and start again.

Being able to haul up sail and get underway quickly has advantages in situations such as this.

Eventually it will happen, the board will be wobbling and your backside will be stuck out, but you will be moving! You will hear the ripples of water building up into what seems like a tremendous bow wave and the board will be slicing its way through the water. From here on it is just a question of practice to lengthen the distance you can cover between falls.

28

Getting underway *Stand in the mast abeam position with your back to the wind .*

Release the uphaul and, with your mast hand, grip the boom adjacent to the mast.

Holding the boom with your mast hand, drop your sheet hand down to your side.

Rake the rig across your body and twist your shoulders so that the mast nearly touches your shin.

Place your sheet hand on the boom and sheet in (draw boom in).

Steering Now that you have managed to get under way successfully you must be able to steer to change direction and get back to where you started from. You steer by tilting the sail forward towards the bow, or aft towards the stern. This will cause the board to bear away (move away from the wind) or luff up (move into the wind) respectively. Experiment by tilting the sail like this and becoming aware of your change in direction and the need to correct your balance. Always be conscious of the direction of the wind or your steering will be hit and miss.

Tacking As you progress, tacking without getting wet will, if you remember the theory, become an easy flowing movement. To do this first rake back the rig. The board will luff up and

head to wind, causing the sail to shake. Take hold of the uphaul rope and shuffle around the front of the mast. The sail will now be on the other side of the board and the board will have swung round into a new direction. Now rake the rig into the new direction, cross over hands, sheet in and away you go again. Only practice will improve your speed and style, but with this basic ability you will be able to leave the shore, sail out, tack and come back to where you started.

With practice the tack should be turned into a

Sailing close-hauled upwind on a day when it is hot enough to wear only a swimming costume.

continual movement; from sailing close-hauled you go quickly into a luff and with the sail flapping you round the mast, change hands and bear away off in the other direction. As you get better the luff can be speeded up by transferring your weight to the back foot, to get the board head to wind. As you round the mast you can drop your sheet hand onto the mast itself, below or above

Tacking

Top left: *Sail close-hauled on a port tack. Lean the rig back to bring the board head to wind.*

Top right: *Grasp the uphaul with your sheet hand and step round to the front of the mast.*

Above: *Transfer the uphaul to your new sheet hand.*

Above right: *Cross over your new sheet hand with your mast hand and with it grab the boom.*

Right: *Lean the rig to windward, grab the boom with the sheet hand and sheet in. Sail off on your new direction.*

the wishbone and use this to pull the rig forward instead of the uphaul.

Bearing away Tacking enables you to move upwind. In order to move downwind the board has to bear away from the wind. This means raking the rig forward which bears the nose away as the board picks up speed. In light airs this is not too much of a problem and the board can be quite easily borne away onto a very broad reach

and with practice taken into the sailing downwind or running position.

Running This is the most unstable and difficult point of sailing a sailboard. The board is very unstable because there is little to no pressure from the sail for you to lean against. The sail is now directly ahead of you at right angles to the board and you will have to look through the window to see forward. Your feet are placed

Gybing Bear away with your leading foot in front of the mast and with the mast raked forward.

Continue to rake the rig forward and then away from the new direction you want to sail in.

Keep bearing away until the board points dead downwind as shown here.

Release the sheet hand to allow the sail to pass around the front of the board.

Change hand positions before sheeting in, so that you let go with your sheet hand and your old mast hand becomes your new sheet hand.

either side of the daggerboard case and the daggerboard itself is the only damper to the rocking motion of the board.

Steering in this position is achieved by angling the rig away from the direction in which you wish to travel, i.e. if you wish to travel to the right, then the rig should be leant to the left, and vice versa.

Gybing The gybe is the term given to a change of direction on a downwind leg. The idea is to get the sail on the opposite tack without having to bring the board head to wind as with conventional tacking whilst moving upwind.

The first method is known as the stop gybe or power gybe. This is also useful in emergencies as it stops the sailboard instantly. You simply sheet out the sail and push it towards the front of the board and pull it back in again with the other hand. At the same time you allow the nose of the board to swing around. In light airs this is relatively simple and is very effective. However, any strength of wind makes this manoeuvre quite difficult since during the movement the sail will be pointing away from you and flapping in the breeze. So the second method must be practised so that you can cope with stronger breezes.

This involves bearing the board further and further away into the running position, and then

slightly beyond. This means you will in fact be sailing with the clew of the sail forward although travelling in the direction of the new tack.

To do this first rake the sail forward then over to one side (opposite to the intended new direction). Now release the sheet hand and quickly transfer it to the mast as the sail rapidly flips down to leeward. With your new mast hand then quickly bring the rig forward and sheet in onto the new tack.

Sailing a circle With both these manoeuvres, tacking and gybing, you should now be able to sail upwind and downwind. The best way to practise is to sail in a large circle. Sailing upwind in a close-hauled position means sailing as near as possible to 45 degrees to the wind. If you move any further upwind the board would stall. To sail close-hauled bring the mast slowly back until at first it luffs, and the board stops. You have turned too far into the wind, so try again until the board points as near to the general wind direction as possible, but continues to move through the water at a reasonable speed.

Then tack to the opposite close-hauled course. After a while, bear the board off through the beam reach onto a broad reach, then into the running position, then gybe onto the other broad reach, tack back to beam reach then close-hauled and so on. This exercise covers all points of sailing and should be carried out in ever increasing wind strengths.

Sheet in as you sail off on your new course.

OUT ON YOUR OWN

You have your sailboard and you are off to explore the sport on your own for the first time. But first you must be aware of the dangers and the need for safety mindedness.

Safety

Sometime sooner or later something will put you in the position of needing to be rescued, or worse still, having to rescue yourself because nobody is around to help. Many things can and do go wrong, but depending on the circumstances and your ability to cope, you should never be in any real danger if you follow a few simple rules.

To be in difficulties in the first place, you must be sailing in a potentially dangerous situation. So this is a pointer to the first rule: if in doubt about your ability to return to shore – do not go.

Beware the offshore wind   When sailboarders get into trouble it is usally on the sea and the most treacherous of circumstances is when the wind is blowing offshore (from the land out to sea). It is dangerous for a number of reasons. Firstly, an offshore wind flattens the waves to make the sea appear calm and inviting, especially to the beginner. Secondly, close inshore the sea is often sheltered providing what might appear to be ideal conditions for the beginner's first venture out. It is a trap that could prove lethal – 90 per cent of windsurfing rescues occur in situations like this.

Imagine such a situation. You are sailing around close to the shore, practising newly learnt manoeuvres and feeling pretty pleased with your performance. The breeze puffs occasionally and the board makes short, but thrilling spurts ahead. Your confidence grows and next time the sailboard surges you bear off and leave the shore a little further behind in the search for more excitement. The gentle puff becomes a sharp gust, the rig feels as if it has tripled in power and suddenly you are yanked up and over and into the sea. You have just experienced your first 'catapult'. Undeterred, you get back on the board.

Now you have to get back towards the shore, but it is not quite so easy. Away from the shore it is much more breezy and there are not so many lulls between the puffs. Not only is the wind stronger and more constant, it is colder too.

The rig behaves as though it is heavier and the wind keeps changing direction sharply. One minute you are sailing straight back to where you came from and the next you can only manage to sail parallel to the shore. Then for no logical reason you begin to fall, just like when you were learning for the first time. As you get more and more cold and your muscles begin to ache you realize how much worse things would be if you were not wearing a wet-suit.

Self rescue   If you find yourself in the situation described above – give up, it is time to start paddling back to shore. Collapse the rig as you

Sailing out on your own for the first time is an exciting event, but beware of the dangers.

If disaster strikes and your rig collapses (above), use your daggerboard or your arms to paddle back to shore.

were shown at the school, undo the outhall, roll the sail up to the mast and tie it securely so that the sail does not drag in the water. Now tie the other end of the boom to the mast and lay the entire rig on the board. Now lie on top face down and paddle back to shore. The main thing you have to worry about now is fatigue. When your arms tire try sitting on the board and using your daggerboard as a paddle.

Obviously, if there are any other boats or sailboards about then get a tow. You should not be completely alone anyway since sailing that way is a dangerous occupation at your stage. Even if there are people around it is possible they will not have seen you – so continue paddling. If you do find you are going to be unnoticed and it is a long way back to shore, you should consider abandoning the rig.

The universal distress signal for board sailors, is to wave both arms up and down over your head to try and attract attention. There are also other safety aids available to the cautious sailor, such as a collapsible paddles that fit up the inside of the mast, and waterproof flares that strap to the leg. A harness with a back pack can be useful for carrying spare bits of line, flares etc.

But the safest thing of all is your own common sense – try not to get into trouble in the first place. These are some basic rules:

1. Always tell somebody you are out and where you are.
2. Try and sail with others, preferably in a club with rescue facilities.
3. Check your equipment before sailing.
4. Wear a wetsuit if you are likely to get cold.
5. Be especially careful in an offshore wind, or better still do not sail in one.
6. Check the weather forecast with your local coastguard.
7. Inform the coastguard of your intentions.
8. Watch others on the water and do not be shy about using a smaller sail.

Equipment failure   This is a serious cause of rescue incidents among board sailors. It might help to illustrate this by describing something that happened to an experienced board sailor recently.

He decided to extend his trip to a run out to the buoy standing about 5km (3 miles) offshore. That was the first mistake – he had not warned anyone of his intentions. The second was to sail off alone and the third was being over confident in his abilities.   Ten minutes after rounding the buoy there was a loud crack and he was pitched into the sea. The mast had snapped clean in two. He was still a long way from shore, in quite a heavy sea and with a long paddle ahead. He folded up the sail and using the short end of the mast paddled canoe-like towards shore. An hour's paddling later he eventually landed some distance from where he had started.

What this story illustrates is that anything can happen, and at any time, however experienced or well prepared you might be. When sailing in coastal waters never become over confident. Always sail with others. Check and double check equipment. And always assume the worse could still happen. Favourite points for disaster are masts, booms and universal joints, all can fail unexpectedly and are impossible to replace from spare parts carried in the back pack and all will land you in considerable trouble if you are any distance from the shore.

Clothing

Wetsuits Even on the warmest summer days, the repeated and inevitable soakings in the sea, will make you cold and uncomfortable. The effects of the wind and the spray evaporating off your body will cause a further loss in body heat. A wetsuit, therefore, is vital.

There are dozens of different brands on the market many of which are designed specifically with windsurfing in mind. The best combination is the long john and bolero two part suit.

The long john covers the legs and upperbody leaving the arms bare from the shoulder. The bolero is a short jacket. Zips are an advantage as they make removal that much easier when the suit is wet. The suit should fit firmly all over with no gaps between the suit and the skin, but not be so tight as to restrict movement or breathing.

Most suits are made of a synthetic cellular material called foam neoprene, which is lined with nylon. Air trapped in the expanded foam layer provides insulation from the cold.

Drysuits Recently another weapon in the fight against the cold has been introduced – the drysuit. This keeps you completely dry with the aid of special rubber seals at the neck, arms and feet. These suits can be worn over ordinary clothes and are very efficient, but can become stifling in warm weather.

The most popular clothing for windsurfing is the long john and bolero combination. Boots specially made for windsurfing often provide better grip than bare feet.

Hats A lot of body heat is lost through the head, so a woollen cap or wetsuit hat can be very effective. But do not allow the ears to be covered as it then becomes more difficult to detect the wind and maintain balance.

Gloves Many a hardened board sailor has been seen howling with pain as the dreaded 'hot hurts' set in. This is what happens as circulation returns to the numb fingers of bare hands in the depths of winter. The perfect wetsuit glove has yet to be invented. Anything between your hands and the boom interferes with your grip but household rubber gloves are one solution. They are cheap, reasonably effective and give a good grip.

Shoes When buying special windsurfing shoes always check their flexibility. There are several cheaper brands on the market which are far too rigid and can produce painful blisters after only a few hours' sailing. However, there are some excellent boots available which actually improve on the grip given by bare feet. They also provide good protection against stubbed toes and knocked ankles. Wetsuit socks, when worn on their own, tend to wear out quickly and give way under pressure, but they are excellent when worn inside a pair of simple tennis shoes.

Transporting the sailboard

Most board owners take their boards to the beach on the roofracks of their cars. Trolley wheels can be useful for taking the board up to the water's edge, especially if the tide goes out a long way or the road is some distance from the water.

Most boards are light and can be easily lifted onto the roofrack by one person. The shape of the board and its lack of wind resistance make transport relatively simple if a few rules are obeyed.

Short journeys If you are going to the nearby beach or reservoir and you do not, therefore, have to travel for any great distance, any reasonable roofrack will do the job. It is easy to just rope the rig and board onto the rack with the sail already on the mast and folded back to the mast tip and the boom in place. The sail will flap in the breeze, but this should not matter too much as long as you do not travel at any great speed.

Avoid using elasticated bungy cords. The

elastic can pull through the metal hook and the board is then liable to blow off the roof.

Longer journeys As a board sailor you are likely to do a lot of travelling which will bring you into contact with all sorts of people and places. Do your utmost to make things easy for yourself and prepare things carefully for each journey.

The roofrack The most popular roofrack is the ladder rack variety, which is simply two bars secured to the car roof. With these you can carry two or even more boards and their rigs. There are more expensive purpose-built racks, some of

To carry the sail over the head, support the boom in one hand and the mast in the other with the rig pointing into the wind. Then throw the rig forward into the water with the mast foot upwind.

which have locking devices – worth considering today because of the high number of boards that are stolen from car roofs.

Fix the board to the rack quite simply with ropes or with special strap kits that you can buy quite easily. Road travel is made easier with mast and sail bags and board bags. You will probably find the best way to carry the board to be the standard nose down, forward facing position, but you should experiment with the manner in which the board or combination of boards is carried.

Carrying the board If you are on your own it can be difficult to load and unload the board.

Try approaching the car from the rear, placing the nose on the rear of the rack, and then sliding the board foward and onto the rack. To carry the board on your own, place one hand in the daggerboard case and the other in the universal slot – the board is usually balanced at about this point. If there are two of you, then it is easier to load and unload a vehicle – one at either end of the board.

As mentioned earlier there are all sorts of aids to help you carry the board and rig to the water's edge. One is a strap arrangement that acts like a sling over the shoulder and supports both the board and the rig, but you need to be very strong to support it. It is always easier to get the board

To carry the board put one hand in the daggerboard case and the other in the mast foot slot – most boards are balanced around this point. With practice you will carry the board easily.

to the water when you are fresh and looking forward to a day's sport, but at the end of a strenuous day's sailing the board can seem twice its original weight.

Launching

Getting the board to the water is one thing; getting it launched is another. The best place for beginners to windsurf is a reservoir where launching is comparatively simple. Put the rig together making certain it is adjusted properly and that the mast foot fits the board. Carry it over your head and put it into the water. Then carry the board with the daggerboard in place out to the rig and then assemble the board and rig. In the case of deep water, get on the board, paddle to the rig and assemble. It is best to choose a shore where the wind is blowing in from an angle of about 45 degrees so that any small wavelets do not make the board too unstable initially. (The first five minutes on the water are always shaky however good you get.)

Launching the board into the sea, especially in waves, requires a little more speed of action to avoid damage to masts and sails. Even relatively small waves have surprising power and can easily snap a mast. So you must learn to give waves the respect they deserve. (See page 48, Launching in surf.)

Slide the daggerboard into the case in the board. Make sure that the mast foot is a good fit.

When you have got both board and rig into the water, plug the mast into the board with the rig downwind of the board. Try to gain extra distance from the shore.

This is an alternative method of launching the sailboard. Hold the board under one arm and hold the rig by the uphaul.

To launch off the beach, make sure everything is ready and place the board facing forward at the water's edge. Take the rig over the head (assuming the wind is blowing onshore), and with one hand on the mast and the other supporting the boom hold the mast at right angles to the wind, or parallel to the water's edge. At this stage the rig should be at the same angle to the wind that you want when setting off, i.e. if the wind is westerly then the mast tip should be pointing east, with the clew of the sail trailing.

Wade into the sea to as far beyond the wave-break point as is possible, then launch the rig as far forward as you can by throwing it. Get back to the board quickly and, with the daggerboard in place, launch the board positioning yourself on it to the windward side of the rig. Now plug in the universal joint, paddling forward a little to gain as much distance between you and the shore as possible. Bring the rig downwind and slightly behind you, then haul up the rig and away you go.

IN MODERATE WINDS

Having learned the basics of windsurfing you probably will have developed a thirst for action in stronger winds. First you will need to develop your confidence.

By the time you are ready to sail in moderate winds you should have spent a hundred or so hours on the water during which time you will probably have caught the occasional gust of wind. Now you have become more proficient your hard-earned skills should enable you to perform more confidently in faster windspeeds.

The ability to 'handle it' does not come overnight but with practice, practice and more practice. In your early days of sailing on flat water in light winds, you will have practised sailing all points of the 'circle' at the Windsurfing school. You should now be doing this quite fluently: the tacks are happening faster and so are the gybes, and though running downwind is probably still difficult you need not worry because it is not such a vital skill at this stage. Some days, however, the wind has probably proved too much and you have had to be content with watching the 'experts' doing some high speed windsurfing.

Your first few attempts at launching in these conditions will probably be unsuccessful. If you manage to launch the board you may find yourself catapulting over the front. Most board sailors learn to cope with moderate winds by gaining experience in a wind of force 2-3. As the wind force slowly increases they find themselves being able to cope with the more difficult conditions. This is the way you will improve far more than by getting out in already moderate conditions.

The term 'moderate' refers to winds with a force of 3-4 on the **Beaufort scale**. You will find such winds very plesant to sail in. The wind is strong enough to support your weight and the sensation of hanging out with your body hovering just above the surface of the waves brings an excitement not experienced before.

There is no comparison between windsurfing in light weather and in moderate winds. The first can seem little more than an interesting balancing excercise, whilst the second is an exciting combination of co-ordinated body movements and the action of wind and water. This exhilaration of speeding over the surface of the water has produced such telling slogans as 'Water skiing without the boat' and 'Sailing with sensation'.

To get the most out of moderate winds it is vital that you practise. The key to sailing in these conditions is *feeling right* – watch other board sailors and look out for the ones who look good. See how their feet are positioned on the board, and copy the ways that they hold the boom. When the wind has blown up so much that you feel unable to handle it, practise on land. If you can manage to get the sail sheeted in on dry land and feel that you could get under way, then you should find that with the momentum of the board it is less difficult on water.

As wind speeds increase, so do the demands on your skills.

Getting under way

This is the hardest part. All the techniques you may have mastered in the earlier chapter have to be virtually relearned. You have to apply more strength to raise the rig clear of the water in stronger winds. Bend at the knees, use your thigh muscles and lean back with your back straight making your weight break the mast tip clear of the water. Ensure that the clew is kept out of the water because if it dips the sail will fill with wind and the strain will pull the uphaul out of your hands and you will be back where you started!

Sheeting in is the most critical manoeuvre. It can either catapult you over the front or bring the board with its nose to wind causing you to fall in backwards. Go through the usual procedure: mast abeam and cross hands. Now rake the mast well to windward and forward, grab the boom with your sheet hand to ensure that you neither fall in the water backwards nor flip over the front of the board. Be prepared for a few duckings – this is not the easiest of manoeuvres.

Top: *For sailing upwind, place your feet either side of the daggerboard case and behind the mast foot.*

Above: *For sailing off the wind place your feet further apart and further aft.*

Various handholds suit different people. Experiment with any of the holds shown below to find which is the most comfortable for you. The two top illustrations are the most popular.

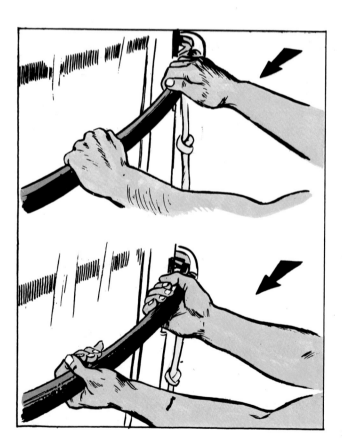

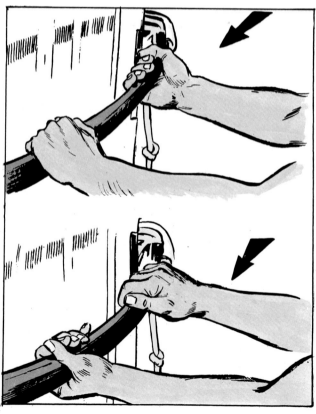

Try and try again, alternating your practice on the land and on the water – eventually you will get under way successfully. Watch the experts and you will notice that sometimes when they take a spill they leave the sail clear. They then try and start off again from the water using the sail to pull themselves clear. Developing the confidence to do this sort of thing is essential for successful windsurfing – but it is a stumbling block. (See page 68, Water start.)

When you do eventually get moving you will probably find yourself hanging on desperately with legs sprawled wide apart, one foot way in front of the mast causing the board to nose dive and the other foot way back and tending to lift off the board with the stronger gusts. Your hands will be outstretched and too far apart, but you will be moving and that is the main thing.

Fortunately, the more you practise, the easier it becomes. Soon you can start concentrating on style. The main points to watch are to keep your feet behind the mast foot and your hands placed evenly either side of the centre of effort on the boom. (This is the point at which it is possible to hold the boom with only one hand.)

The first direction everyone takes is a close reach, and once you have mastered this the next thing is to practise tacking again. At speed everything has to be performed faster – as the sail goes back the board comes up head to wind fairly quickly, so you have to learn to be fast on your feet. As you rake the mast back try to get one foot around the other side of the mast, then hop around quickly holding the mast under the boom instead of the uphaul.

Sailing upwind in moderate conditions presents no real problems, but returning downwind does. To do this you will need to bear away, and as this becomes quite difficult in stronger winds, this should be the next exercise.

Bearing away

You already know the theory and you know that the mast should be well forward, but in stronger winds you have to lean back in order to counter the pull from the sail. You will have to crouch quite low and put your lead foot forward of the mast, just long enough to get the board on its way without dipping its nose. Then, still crouching, swing your body to move the rig forward. Now there is a critical moment when you must sheet out and swing back – if you oversheet you will fall in backwards. If you sheet out too soon the board will not bear off, but will head back up again. If you fail to sheet out soon enough you

This board sailor is sailing close-hauled and is using the overhand hold.

will catapult over the front of the board.

Once the board is on its way there is tremendous acceleration. This is the fastest point of sailing and to maintain it you will need to move both feet back down the board, keep the rig well forward and sheet in and out to counter the increase and decrease in the speed of the wind and board.

Gybing

Bearing away is the forerunner to the gybe which is now quite a difficult movement with the increased speed. Follow the same procedure and, keeping the rig well forward, move it over to windward until the board has passed through the **eye of the wind**. (The direction of the true wind.) Now jump to the back of the board. This will make the nose start to swing up in the direction of the new tack. Now release the sheet hand letting the sail flip round the front of the board.

43

While this is happening, switch hands at the mast. As the board luffs (tries to point head to wind), pull the rig well forward and stay borne away on the new tack.

Gybing in moderate winds: *Bear away onto a broad reach, as the board passes through the eye of the wind, release your sheet hand allowing the sail to flip round the front of the board and put you on a new tack.*

Running

The excitement of free sailing in moderate airs with the strong support of the sail.

When gybing you must have passed a point when you were running dead before the wind. Running or sailing dead downwind is where the board is at its most inefficient. You are simply being pushed along by the wind so there is no need for the daggerboard apart from providing you with stability. Getting onto the run in stronger winds is a natural progression from bearing away and means using the same controls except that you may need to stand further back down the board than in lighter conditions.

In waves you will find yourself moving up and down the board in order to counter nose dives. You steer in the same way as discussed in earlier chapters. Running in any sort of wind is the most difficult point of sailing for the board sailor for reasons already explained. When doing it try and remain as relaxed as possible with your knees slightly bent.

IN FRESHER WINDS

The term 'fresh breeze' may sound quite innocent. On the Beaufort Scale 'fresh breeze' refers to winds between force four and force six, and windsurfing in these conditions presents a whole new set of board handling problems and a whole new world of thrills.

Sailing in winds of any strength requires a high degree of competence and the board sailor, of course, needs to be well prepared. For high wind fun, two areas have to be looked at – smaller sails and daggerboards. Smaller sails are necessary because larger sails take too much wind in fresh conditions and make the sailboard impossible to handle. The best way of deciding which sail to use, storm or marginal sail, is to set up the rig on the beach and try it there.

The problem with daggerboards in fresh winds is that increased speed tends to make the daggerboard try to hydrofoil to the surface, or **plane** (see below).

Daggerboards

If you have sailed in anything approaching a force four, you will probably have noticed the hydrofoil effect by now: as the board speed increases, especially when sailing off the wind on a broad reach, the nose of the board seems to lift too high and feels as if there is an air pocket under the board. The board, then, begins to roll from side to side, flips up onto one rail and tips you in to the water. If you are sailing upwind the

Sailing in fresher winds is a challenge, but it can be dangerous.

hydrofoil effect is not quite so bad unless you are exceptionally light, in which case the board will 'rail' that much earlier. The railing effect can be countered by pulling the daggerboard half way out of its case, but this also has the effect of moving the centre of resistance forward, exactly the opposite to what is required in stronger winds.

Sailboards with swivel daggerboards are better equipped for fresh wind sailing; to counter hydrofoiling tilt the board aft slightly. But off the wind in very fresh conditions you may have to pull even this type of daggerboard. So here is what to do.

Pulling the daggerboard Get the board's nose into a position where it is pointing considerably off the wind, with the sail luffing in the mast abeam position. With the mast hand still in place, reach down with the sheet hand, pull out the daggerboard and sling it over your arm by the strap. Be careful not to drop the rig or allow the nose of the board to point back upwind; let the rig go as far forward as possible before sheeting in and leaning back. If you do this correctly the board will leap forward as water fountains up from the daggerboard case.

You will skip from wavetop to top with little spurts of spray gushing from the slot as the board touches down – an experience all of its own.

Storm dagger An alternative to sailing without the daggerboard is to use a storm daggerboard. This is much smaller and more swept back to bring the centre of resistance back. It is less likely to hydrofoil, but does not give very good upwind performance. Its main use is for sheer fun: messing about in waves and running the board up the beach.

Launching in heavy surf

Having the necessary equipment is one thing, but being able to launch and use it is another. By now you should be pretty competent. If you are not you should not attempt to go out when it is 'all hair and teeth'.

But there always has got to be a first time, and this is it. Let us assume you have got the force four barrier mastered; you can tack and gybe well, and sail all points of the circle with only the occasional fall. You have mastered sailing without the daggerboard and tasted the thrills of higher wind – and now you are looking for the ultimate.

On the nearby beach pavilion the flags are standing out straight, on the water there are white caps and the waves are crashing on to the beach. The beach is relatively shallow, so there is a reasonable distance between each wave but there are still a couple of hundred metres of 'white water' to negotiate.

Watch how the real expert slides down the beach with his Windsurfer Rocket, its footstraps

and upswept nose promising exciting action. The mast has a high clew marginal which he sheets in tight. He adjusts his harness lines, connects his mast foot leash and is ready to get underway.

He then moves to the back of the board, picks up its stern in one hand, and with the other holds the rig by the boom. He pushes the board in front of him until there is enough water to clear the storm daggerboard and casually drops the tail of the board. Stepping on, he sheets in, glides his feet into the straps and hooks up the harness. Ten seconds later he is airborne.

The best way to learn is to watch other people and then try it yourself. To do this you have to sail with others, and this guarantees not only that you are learning all the time, but also that you are safe in the company of people who know what they are doing.

On a steeply shelving beach where the waves dump one after the other at very short intervals, the launch method described above will not work. Launching on a beach such as this is made additionally difficult by the undertow caused by the waves' breaking action.

When leaving the beach in extreme conditions, beware of any groynes and rocks that will make return difficult – even if they are some way downwind. It is surprising how little time it takes if you are struggling at the water's edge to be dragged off down the coast by a combination of tide and current.

Having launched and sailed the first hundred

To launch a sailboard in surf or from a shallow beach support it by the tail of the board and the uphaul. Push the board into the water and jump on. It is a tricky method, but quick.

When sailing in strong winds the mast bends, the sail is distorted and air is spilled from the sail. When this happens the rig loses its efficiency and becomes difficult to control.

Tackling surf conditions can be dangerous and costly. Try to avoid the sort of wipe out shown here.

metres or so it is not uncommon to find that you can barely hold the rig up; perhaps because of sheer nervous exhaustion. If this happens, sail out beyond the breakers, drop the rig and sit on the board for a few minutes. Next time you will probably find you can sail for some time without any trouble. A warmup sail, which is what has been effectively described here, is essential. It livens the muscles and keys up your performance. Some people run through a few exercises on the beach before launching; others take a brisk jog, especially in winter.

Sailing technique

Upwind in a blow   Some of the problems that occur as the wind strength increases have already been mentioned, but without reference to particular points of sailing. This is because the forces acting are different in each case although the remedy might be the same.

If you try to make ground upwind in something approaching a force six, say, you are beset with difficulties. If you are using a smaller sail and storm daggerboard your general sailing performance might be good, but your windward performance is not. This is because, firstly, the reduced size of the daggerboard fails to prevent leeway (sidewards movement downwind) and, secondly, a smaller sail does not sail close enough to the wind. If you are still struggling with a full size sail, because the strength of the wind has caught you by surprise or you simply do not own a smaller rig, then you are likely to experience quite a few problems.

It will be extremely difficult to set the sail to start with. The sail will continually luff at the head, and in gusts, point head to wind, making it

When sailing in strong winds move your hands back down the boom keeping your arms straight and move your feet more to the back of the board.

If you are suddenly caught by a lull when sailing in strong winds, crouch low. This will bring your body back closer to the board's centre.

virtually impossible to bear off sufficiently to make forward movement. When the board does move the pressure on the daggerboard caused by the leeward movement of the board, will cause the board to ride up on its rail. With all this happening, how on earth do people still manage to sail? The answer is, few people do, but it is possible: this is how:

Upwind in heavy weather with normal sail To work upwind in these conditions you have to develop an action, sometimes called the 'body twist'. When a stray gust hits you, you roll up into an upright position. Twist from the hip, keeping the board pointing in the direction in which you wish to travel and keep hold the boom

with both hands. Luff the sail for a moment, then twist back again, sheeting in. This technique can be carried out while you are hooked in. Its big advantage is that you are at one with the rig and simply pivoting on your feet.

Space your hands evenly well down the boom because the centre of effort moves back with the increase in wind. If possible your feet should be

When sailing off the wind in fresh breezes, the board will be made easier to control if you pull out the daggerboard. It can then be slung over the shoulder.

behind the daggerboard. The board should be kept borne away by your weight leaning forward to a position at which you are best balanced. If you are fairly light, you are likely to have trouble here and may have to use your front foot to continually kick the nose of the board off the wind.

If you point too much into the wind the daggerboard will stall. But if you sail too far off the wind the daggerboard will plane with the increased speed. You are aiming at a very fine line between these two extremes.

Sailing off the wind   Sailing off the wind is fast and furious, with occasional thrills and spills. It is not nearly so difficult as making ground upwind and you can cover the same distance in a tenth of the time. However, it is not without its difficulties.

If you have problems maintaining balance when running downwind, it will help if you sit or kneel on the board. Try to anticipate gusts and lulls.

Downwind   Running off the wind is always as difficult but if you have mastered running in all other conditions you will find it slightly easier in a blow as there is enough power in the sail to allow you to lean back.

Problems do occur when sailing in large waves. If the board catches a wave, it can out-accelerate the wind and make the sail lose power. This gives the board sailor nothing to hang onto or steer with and if the board buries its nose in the back of the next wave it may cause him to fall off.

As the wind strength increases to around force 3 running downwind becomes slightly easier with the extra power in the sail to support you. Over force 3 running becomes increasingly difficult.

Fast sailing in a good breeze.

You can be pulled forward and over the front of the board by a gust when bearing off, or you might be caught off-balance just after a lull. The skeg might break out of the water at very high speed and cause the board to bounce from one chine to the other – this is known as 'chine dancing!' This can build up and throw you off.

Another problem is that the 'non-slip' surface on the deck can become too wet and slippery.

This boardsailor is in perfect control although leaping off a wave.

When running or reaching in waves it helps to move around on the board. Surfers in action on the face of waves have to move around on the surfboard and likewise this footwork can be a great help to the board sailor. The theory is that you help a board onto the wave's face by moving your weight forward (if you sheet in hard or 'pump' the sail at the same time you will accelerate faster), then the surfing action can be prolonged by moving aft. The beauty of strong wind sailing is that there is always a constant source of power to fall back against when you are running around on the board. The thrills of high wind windsurfing combined with surfing in waves is almost the ultimate in this sport.

Windsurfing in strong winds is physically very demanding, but a labour-saving device has already been contrived to make it easier – the harness.

The harness

The most successful harness, and one readily used today, was developed in Hawaii. It is a sort of shoulder waistcoat with adjustable straps and a metal hook at mid-chest height. A loop of rope is attached to the boom which you simply swing up into the open ended hook and lean back. To release it you pull in with your arms and let the loop fall out of the hook.

The Hawaii harness has been improved over the years and now has a back pack and a quick release buckle, which is essential. The quick release buckle enables you to get out of the harness in a hurry and on no account should you consider buying a harness that does not have one.

Bouyancy aids and harnesses are being combined in one unit now. (On some inland waterways you are required by law to wear a buoyancy aid.)

A harness line is comprised of a rope and two tapes. Wind the tapes two full turns round the boom about 60cm (2ft) apart and knot the rope through both eyelets. When you are hooked up and leaning against the harness line, your hook should be about 20cm (8ins) away from the boom. Too tight and it is difficult to unhook. Too lose and it will not take the strain.

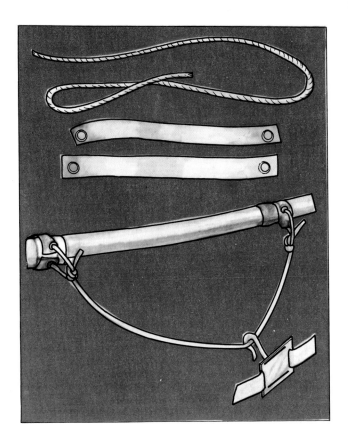

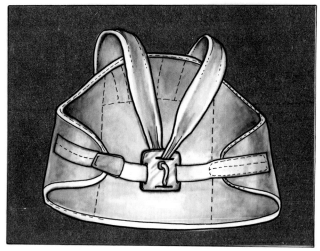

The Hawaiian harness has an open hook and a quick release buckle.

Wave jumping

Riding down the face of waves in strong or moderate wind is one thing; but to career up the face of a wave and leap clear at the top is another. Many feel this to be the ultimate in windsurfing experiences.

Unfortunately, there are very few places where perfect wave jumping conditions exist. Ideally you require a beam or broad reach straight into the oncoming wave. Most of the European coastline only produces waves along the shore line, built up by the wind that exists at the moment, and therefore the wind and waves are travelling in the same direction. A beam reach in those conditions only produces a shallow ramp diagonally up the face of an oncoming wave which does not produce the spectacular jumps such as are possible in the board sailors' paradise, Hawaii.

The Hawaiians developed wave jumping as a sport, and naturally they developed the boards on which it is best performed. It is possible to jump waves on any board, but the foot-straps on a special wave jumping board make control for the experienced sailor very easy.

What you need for wave jumping, apart from the waves, is an upswept board with footstraps, a marginal sail with a high clew and a harness. How you jump is a simple matter of pointing the board at the wave and lifting off. How you land is the problem.

As a sailboard becomes airborne it has a tendency to drop its windward rail. Without straps it is nearly impossible to stay on.

Safety precautions

As well as the normal precautions like sailing with others, informing coastguards and so on, ther are one or two other things that must be observed when windsurfing in fresher winds.

The mast leash A safety leash between the board and the rig is a good idea in most conditions, but it is something that sailboarders do not always like or bother with. In surf at sea, it is a must. The likelihood of your board being swept

away from you after a fall is much greater in breaking waves, and your board is your life raft. The least you can do to slow its progress is to fit a line between it and the rig.

Respect Have respect for the elements. It is so easy as you become better, to be so confident as to believe you are absolutely in charge. Wrong! Water and wind especially on the sea are very powerful and unforgiving elements when taken too lightly. Breaking waves contain tremendous power, as do the undertow and rip currents. You can easily be knocked unconscious by a rock or your own rig if you come off your board.

Be especially careful when launching: never put the board between you and a wave – always stand to one side. If you get into real trouble at the water's edge, get yourself out first; you can always go back for the board and rig.

Pulling out the daggerboard to prevent the hydrofoil effect in fresh winds. Water spurts up through the daggerboard case.

RACING

No sooner had Drake and Schweitzer built two
wind-surfers than they were racing them – eventually
you may wish to do the same. Racing will test
every one of your newly acquired skills – and demand
that you acquire more.

Yacht racing is a very old sport and there are
well-established ways of racing sailboats against
each other. All that is needed is a little organiza-
tion, a few buoys to sail around, some people to
handle entry details, make certain no one cheats,
and that no one comes to any harm.

A lot of these facilities are now being made
available to the board sailor thanks to a lot of
work put in by board sailing organizations. Originally there was only the Windsurfer sailboard
and hence the Windsurfer Class Association
which existed for competition between Windsurfer owners. The great variety of sailboards
now available has led to a need for more organizations to stage competitions. So if you are
interested in racing, first check that your board
has an organized owners' assocation. This is
likely if it is a Windsurfer, Windglider, Mistral,
Sailboard, Sea Panther or Dufour Wing. If you
have one of these you can learn to race on equal
terms in what is known as a 'One Design' competition in which all the boards are the same.

If your sailboard is not one of these you can
race in the so-called 'Open' Class in which any
make of board is welcomed, provided it falls

*Sailboarders competing in an Open Class regatta
on a variety of different makes of board.*

within a restricted sail and board measurement
specification, as laid down by the International
Board Sailing Association (IBSA).

If you want to race join an assocation. You will
receive a newsletter giving dates, times and
places of events and a magazine with interesting
articles to help you with your tactics. It will also
give information on the complex rules structure
which the rest of this chapter will serve to break
the surface of.

What you will need

Having joined an association they will be quick
to advise you to insure yourself and your equipment. As far as special equipment is concerned,
you should find a standard sailboard with a
regatta sail is still perfectly adequate for racing.
A harness will be a great help since the races can
last for an hour or more and are quite strenuous.

It may also be necessary to have a buoyancy
aid on hand since racing often takes place at
Yacht Clubs which insist on personal buoyancy.

Having entered a race you may receive Sailing
Instructions through the post. These may contain terms totally new to you so read a few books
beforehand and you will soon be familiar with
them. Some of them also apply to dinghy and
yacht racing.

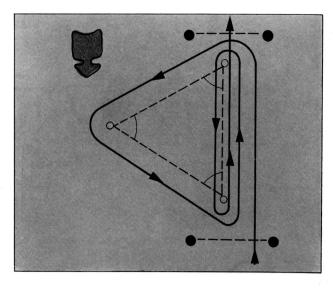

The Olympic course has three beats upwind, two reaches and one run downwind.

The course

Sailboard racing takes place over what is known as the Standard Olympic Triangle course. This course is used throughout most serious yacht and dinghy competitions, and is designed to test the helmsman's skill over all points of sailing. Beating to windward, reaching and running.

A buoy is positioned dead upwind from the starting point (see illustration); another buoy is set at a point at right angles to a line drawn

Top left: *The class flag.* Top right: *The Blue Peter.* Bottom left: *The answering pennant.* Bottom right: *The general recall.*

between the starting point and the windward mark to form a triangle. A third buoy is set just above the starting point to complete the three buoy course. The start line is an imaginary line drawn between a buoy and usually the main mast of the committee boat from where the race is controlled: all the start and finish signals are carried out from here and finishing numbers and order are taken.

The flags

The committee boat is equipped with a system of flags which serve to instruct the fleet as to such details as time delay to the start, postponements, alterations to course etc. Some of these flags ought to be recognized before setting about racing. The first is your **class flag**, which is nor-

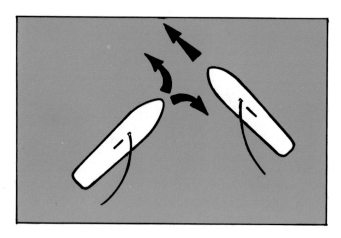

The sailboard on the right is on a starboard tack. The sailboard on the left, since it is on a port tack, must give way to the other sailboard.

mally the initial letter (e.g., the Windsurfer class is flag 'W').

This class flag is hoisted and a signal is sounded exactly ten minutes before the start of the race. Five minutes later the preparatory signal is raised, from which time racing rules begin to apply. This is indicated by hoisting the **Blue Peter** – a white square on a blue background. The start of the race is signalled by another sound signal and the lowering of both these flags.

If the race has to be postponed for a short time, through bad weather, lack of wind or any other reason, another flag called the **answering pennant** is broken out. This is a long red and white striped flag and is hoisted along with a sound signal. When it is lowered another sound signal is made which allows at least one more minute before the ten minute flag is hoisted again.

If before the start, competitors have strayed over the line, the whole fleet may be recalled. This **general recall** is announced by sound signals and the hoisting of a yellow and blue triangular pennant.

Two other flags which are plain red and green indicate how the course is laid out. The most usual arrangement is with the reaching buoy or 'wing mark' to port (left). This is a port hand course and is signalled by a red flag. A starboard (right) hand course is marked by a green flag. Port and starboard are used to describe everything in terms of direction of travel, and the position of the sail in relation to the board.

Port and starboard tacks These describe the direction in which a board is sailing, whether in a race or on open water. A sailboard on a port tack gives way to one on a starboard tack. Here is an

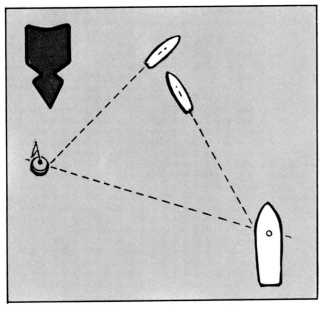

If two sailboards leave from different ends of the start line at the same time and the one on the port tack crosses above the one on the starboard tack, this suggests the port end is favoured by the wind.

easy way to realize which tack you are on: if you are sailing forward with your right hand forward or next to the mast, then you are on a starboard tack. Some sailboards have the boom coloured green on this side to indicate starboard.

The port and starboard rule is known as the 'fundamental rule' which everyone who races must know about in order to avoid total confusion. Even so, boards still collide, and when they do the boat in the wrong must perform a penalty. In dinghy racing this used to be as severe as retiring from the race, but with sailboards the

sailor must perform a 720 degree turn, that is tack and gybe the board twice. This penalty must be performed for infringements of right of way rules – collisions when rounding marks, overtaking etc.

The race

Before the race starts there is a skippers' meeting. The course is described on a board and any special conditions are explained. Wind direction and tide, weather forecast, colour of buoys, which mast of the committee boat is the start line, are all points that should come out at this meeting. If they do not or you are unsure of something, then ask!

Start and first beat At your first regatta you are not likely to star but there are certain things that if spotted can give you an advantage.

First, you must know the start routine: the ten minute gun is followed by the five minute gun, both flags drop, the start gun fires and you are off.

At the start the majority of the fleet will be lined up along the start line on a starboard tack. As they sail off some immediately move ahead while others, their sails shielded from the wind by the sails of other competitors, sail slower and slower.

Soon after the start many sailboards at the starboard end of the line tack to port in search of

The leeward sailboard is in the wind shadow of the sailboard to windward. This can be used as a tactic when racing.

'clear air'. This is one way of escaping the effects of wind shadow at the start. It is only possible to do this however, if no one is approaching on starboard from behind you.

Start line favoured end When the race committee lay a start line, inevitably one end of the line is more favourable to start from than the other. One end is either nearer the windward mark, or the wind is favouring one end rather than the other as it changes direction. You can discover this in two ways. The first is the easiest: if you have a friend with you, get him to sail close

hauled away from one end of the line as you sail from the other. Sail on opposite tacks towards the middle of the line. The one who sails ahead of the other when you meet has obviously left the favoured end.

The other method is not quite so easy. First you have to position the board in line with the start line and hold the sail in the mast abeam position. The sail will point more to one end

Last minute preparations in the tense moments before a race.

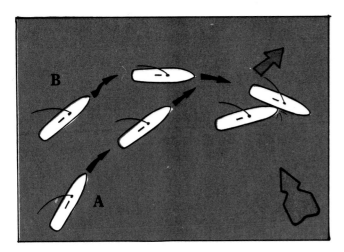

*Sailboard **A** is attempting to overtake **B** and steal his wind supply. **B** has the right to luff (turn into the wind). If this resulted in a collision **A** would have to sail two complete circles as a penalty.*

than the other. Start from the opposite end to which it points.

First beat   The first mark is upwind, so you have to sail as fast and as close to the wind as possible. The wind is inevitably changing direction slightly so try and spot the times when the

*If sailboard **A** manages to bring his stern level with **B**'s mast **A** can call 'mast abeam' which ends **B**'s luffing rights. Both sailboards would then resume a proper course to the next mark.*

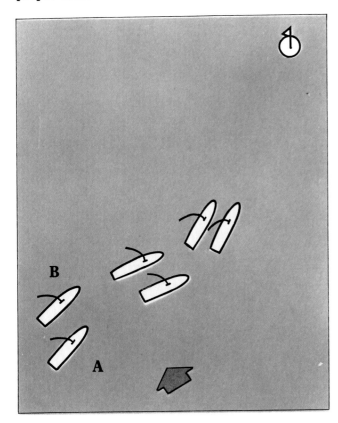

wind is favouring a tack which brings you nearer to the mark.

If your position is challenged from behind, you can use all sorts of legitimate tricks. You can place your challenger in your wind shadow, the area immediately behind and to leeward of you. If you can look over your shoulder, down the clew of your sail and see your opponent, he is sailing in your 'dirty' air. This will force him further and further downwind of you, making it impossible for him to point as high, since the air-stream is already curved and disturbed as it leaves your sail. On the other hand, if you are sailing in someone's dirty air, the same will be happening to you, so tack away.

You can use the right of way rules to force other boats to tack away and below you at such

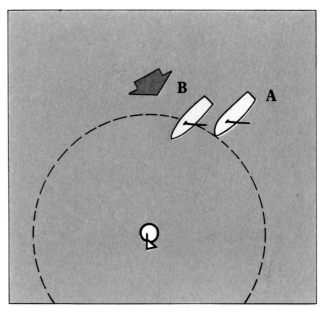

*Sailboard **B** has established an overlap just as **A** enters an imaginary circle which is two board lengths from the mark. This entitles **B** to sea room as he rounds the mark.*

critical moments as approaches to the mark. Once around the mark you can then kick back the daggerboard or, if the wind is stronger than force 3–4, pull it out and career off down the reach.

Reach and gybe   Racing down the reach is very exciting and offers the chance to make real gains against opponents. You actually pass them going in the same direction and can see the results instantly, rather than waiting to meet them on the next tack before knowing if you are in front or behind. The problem is that as you try and pass the opponent in front, to windward, he will 'luff' you, i.e. sail higher and higher on the wind

to protect his air supply and prevent you over-taking.

Luffing If you are about to be overtaken, and this counts for anywhere on the race course, you have the right to bring your board head to wind if necessary to protect your wind supply. You do not have to give any warning, except during the five minutes leading up to the start. Luffing matches on a reach are a nuisance, they impede your progress and alter your course, but they happen. The moment you are threatened by a competitor trying to overtake to windward bring your rig back sharply and shout 'Up! Up!' and, if possible, touch his board with your own. He will then have to perform a 720 degree turn, since an overtaking or windward boat must keep clear.

However, if he does manage to come along-side and bring his stern level with your mast he can then call 'mast abeam!' which ends your luffing rights.

Mark rounding Always leave as much room as possible when approaching the gybe mark, or

Launching sailboards and getting under-way before a race.

any other for that matter. If you hit a mark when racing you are required to re-round it, avoiding all the other boards, which can be very time consuming. The gybe mark in particular is a disaster area, so special attention should be made to your gybing technique if you are intending to race seriously. If in doubt it is better to perform a stop or power gybe (see page 33) than risking a fall or sailing too far past the mark with a conventional gybe.

The second beat This is carried out in the same manner as the first. Use your tactical ability to its utmost. Cover those sailboards behind you and try to influence those ahead. Use the windshifts and your rights of way. By now you probably realize that racing sailboards is similar to playing a very strenuous game of chess on a moving board.

Pumping Rule 60 of the IYRU and RYA rules

is quite explicit about illegal propulsion, which includes pumping in certain circumstances. Pumping is defined as frequent trimming of the sail, very often in rhythmic motion and can be used to speed up a sailboard on all points of sailing.

In the chapter on waves it was suggested that at the crest of a wave you sheet in hard to help the board plane down its face. This is a perfectly legal area in racing where pumping can be used skilfully and competitively.

The action required to pump a sailboard is basically two-fold. First lean the rig forward and slightly release the sheet hand. The sail fills with air. Then fan the rig back towards you, so 'pumping' the board forward. In conditions described as 'non-planing' it is highly illegal to

The leading sailboard is on a port tack. He must give way to the overtaking sailboard as it is on a starboard tack.

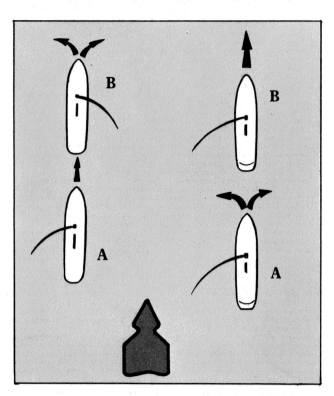

Left: *Sailboard* **A** *is approaching* **B** *on a starboard tack.* **B,** *since he is on a port tack, must keep clear.* Right: *Both sailboards are on the same tack.* **A,** *the overtaking board, must keep clear.*

fan the board along like this, but because the board is so unstable by nature, board sailors have to sheet in and out simply to maintain balance. Naturally, some of the cleverer sailors can fake loss of balance and instability to use the pumping action to gain unfair advantage.

Pumping can also take place on the downwind legs, and be disguised as the natural action required to steer a board down the run. Inevitably there is always great discussion on whether

pumping should be allowed at all, and if not how to outlaw it.

The run The next obstacle is the dead run – and it is where most racing board sailors come to grief. Decide early whether you are going to pull out the daggerboard or swivel it back. And remember this will have the effect of making your sailboard even more unstable.

If you are in control the run is another place where some gains can be made. First check that you are not totally covered by the sails of the boards behind you. Then do your best to cover the sailboard directly in front. As you come up to

This sailboard has hit a mark while rounding it. As a penalty he must sail a full circle round the mark before sailing off.

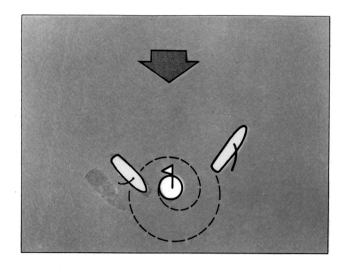

the leeward mark, try for the inside line but take it wide at first and round hard up on the windward side, not leaving any room for an opponent to gain advantage by sneaking upwind of you.

Final beat and finish   At the end of the run you will have rounded the leeward mark twice already, and should have noted each time which direction the wind may have favoured. This final beat should be your best. There is no magical solution which will bring you from your mid-fleet position to first place, but sensible sailing should at least help you maintain your position and with one or two tricks still available to you, perhaps gain a couple of places.

The finish line is either set with the committee

put you at a considerable disadvantage, then you have the right to protest. You do this by telling the competitor at the time, or as soon after it as possible. Then you must inform the committee boat at the end of the race. On the beach you will be given a protest form. You write the details of the incident, state which rules you consider may have been broken and when, the state of the tide, wind, etc, drawn as a sketch.

The whole matter is then heard in front of a protest committee which is usually comprised of three non-participating sailors from the host club. You give evidence in very much the same way as one does in court, backing it up with evidence from any witness you may have procured.

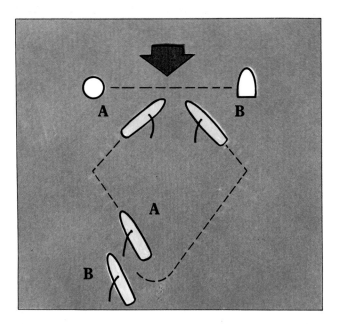

*Sailboards **A** and **B** are approaching the finish line together, but **B** cannot tack until **A** has done so. **A** will finish first.*

*Sailboard **B**, in this illustration, changes from a starboard tack, to port and back to starboard to finish. If both boards cross the line together, **B** will win through being on a starboard tack.*

boat lined up with the windward mark, or as a totally separate line a hundred yards or so further on upwind. Either way, as with the start line, one end of it is likely to be favoured.

The first way to take advantage of this is tactical. If you and another sailboard have been swapping tacks all the way up the last beat, make certain you finish on starboard. The second way is to realize quickly which end of the line is nearest and to sail for it.

Protests

If you consider that another sailboard has infringed the rules, especially in such a way as to

The whole procedure may at first seem repugnant to you, as this is after all only a leisure activity: but this is the wrong way to look at it. It is no use playing any game or entering any serious competition unless there are rules, and as there are rules they must be adhered to. The protest rule, which uses the competitors as a sort of self-policing system, works very well – so do not be afraid to use it.

FREESTYLE AND GAMES

Freestyle and hotdogging are terms borrowed
from skiing to describe tricks which are both gymnastic
and fun to watch. These tricks add a new and
skilful dimension to windsurfing, but you
obviously will need a good grounding in the basics before
you can try them.

A small crowd of curious sunbathers lift their heads to watch as you prepare to put on a free show. You give the mast foot an extra wind of tape and with a much-practised flourish, flip the board onto its edge, put one foot on the daggerboard and 'rail' straight off the sand and into the surf. The sunbathers are sitting up by now, hands shading their eyes. You execute a perfect flare gybe followed by a jump tack. As you approach the beach, you spin to the leeward side of the sail and fold both arms across your chest whilst leaning against the mast. Showing off? Of course you are, but then that is half the fun of the sport.

International competitions

The first major freestyle competition was held at the Windsurfer World Championships in Sardinia in 1977 and was dominated by the Americans. They demonstrated previously unheard of tricks including riding the board on its rail (edge) at a time when most people were still having difficulty sailing the board in its normal position without complicating things further!

A confidently performed head dip, with both feet on the rail, or edge of the board.

Robby Naish, Ken Winner and Matt Schweitzer, astonished the Europeans with their duck tacks, forward rail rides and head dips. In one of the most spectacular displays, Ken Winner performed the pirouette, a forward facing and backward facing rail ride; Robby Naish rode the rail standing inside the wishbone; Matt Schweitzer demonstrated wheelies (the nose of the board is lifted out of the water by standing on the tail), flare gybes and duck spin tacks.

Up until then, most of these routines lacked finish, and falls were not uncommon, but by 1978 it was becoming clear that these tricks could be as stylish as figure skating.

Conditions for freestyle

Conditions should be as near ideal as possible when you are learning tricks: a sunny day in warm water in a force 2-3 suits most people.

The water should obviously be as calm as possible and preferably about a metre deep to minimize tiring climbs on board. Freestyle is best done on flat inland water which, in the summer, is generally warmer than the sea. Freestyle practice will also improve your general board control and confidence as during your many attempts you will find yourself recovering from positions you previously found impossible.

Above: *Start of the head dip.*
Above centre: *Bend your knees and straighten arms until your head touches the water.*
Above right: *Head dip while riding the rail.*

Head dip This was the first acknowledged trick and it is one that will quickly tell you if you have any fear of water! Enjoy the sensation of travelling at some speed with an upside down horizon and blinding spray.

In a freestyle competition this trick is sometimes performed while riding the rail.

Sail on a beam reach in a force 3-4 wind and lean out against the breeze with all your body weight supported by the wind in the sail. Now arch your back and throw your head backwards with your knees bent until your head hits the water.

Water start The water start is often accidentally performed in emergencies when a windward capsize has not been total. (Though the feet may have left the board the rig is still held clear of the water and the backside and trunk are immersed.)

One way to do this deliberately is to stall the board and allow your body to dip into the water whilst keeping the sail clear of the water. Then get your feet back onto the board – the more of your weight on the board, the less effort on the sail to keep you afloat. Help the sail as much as possible by pushing it. When the wind seems strong enough sheet in to lift clear of the water and sail away.

Below left: *Put your feet well onto the board.*
Below centre: *Sheet in to lift you out of the water.*
Below right: *The sail will pull you up into a standing position.*

Leeward side facing sail This is one of the first tricks you should learn after the head dip. It involves simply sailing the board from the wrong side of the sail and pushing against the wind instead of pulling.

It is not that difficult to get into position: start off from the mast abeam position, turn half a circle and face the wind while raking the mast across the body as in a conventional start (but facing the sail and wind). Then lean into the sail and push to sheet in.

An alternative method is to go into a conventional tack, pass the nose of the board through the eye of the wind, then, instead of rounding the mast, simply bring the rig forward again sheeting out slightly as it goes. Then push to sheet in and bear away from the leeward side.

Sailing with your back to the sail on the leeward side. Note that the mast hand is actually on the mast.

In the leeward side facing sail position you have to push against the boom instead of pull.

Back to sail leeward side This is very similar to the previous trick, except the board is sailed with the back to the sail and all the movements have to be thought about harder and with more sensitivity to the wind or you could be thrown forward.

Sail on a close reach to get into position. Luff the sail, put your rear foot to the other side of the mast, then pull the rig forward with the sail still luffing. To do this you will have to lean forward to sheet out and lean back to sheet in. In the gusts you will need to lean harder, and in lulls you will have to be quick to avoid falling into the sail. With practice this can be a very comfortable trick and you will be sailing effortlessly while you lean back against the sail.

Back to sail windward side This is quite a difficult trick because firstly, you cannot see the sail and secondly, your reactions need to be opposite to that of normal sailing.

Sail on a starboard tack on a close reach. Release the mast hand and move the sheet hand up to the mast while turning to face the wind. Reach behind for the boom.

Sailing with your back to the sail on the windward side is difficult – you cannot even see the sail.

Riding the rail Riding the rail is the first real ambition of anyone with freestyle aspirations.

First sail the board on a beam reach on smooth water with the wind blowing around force 2-3. Place your rear foot on the leeward side of the board and try pushing down with it a couple of times. Kneel your forward foot onto the windward side of the board, with the toes hooked under the rail. Pushing with the rear foot, lift up with the front foot. As you do this the board will tilt further and further onto its edge.

For a complete rail, flip the board up with the front foot, and sheet out the sail to prevent the board carrying on over and falling in to leeward. Then sheet in gently to prevent a windward fall.

After you have balanced the board on the rail for a couple of seconds, transfer your front foot initially to the daggerboard, leaving the rear foot on the rear rail. From this stable position other feet combinations can be practised, like both feet on the rail, both on the dagger, or one foot on the skeg and the other on the daggerboard.

Push down with your rear foot and, hooking the instep of your front foot under the rail, flip up the board.

To gain this position, kneel on the instep of your front foot, bringing up your rear foot onto the rail.

With both feet on the rail it is important to stay low until you are confident enough to stand.

As you become more used to the feel of the board you can gradually straighten your legs.

Both feet on the daggerboard is one of the many combinations possible when riding the rail.

Onto the rail, front foot on daggerboard

Getting into the wishbone   This is quite a simple trick, but can be very effective when combined with a rail ride. This is best practised on flat water in a steady breeze.

Simply bend the knees and duck under and into the boom lifting first the rear then the front arms so the boom sits under the armpits. Steer by swaying the body while leaning comfortably back against the wind.

Duck tack First bring the board head to wind as if a normal tack were about to take place. Then, with the sail luffing, throw it forward into the wind (left). As you step under it slide your forward hand back along the boom until the sail is high enough to pass under (centre). Then with your rear hand quickly grab the rig on the new side as you pull the sail back (right). For this entire manoeuvre you must be fast and surefooted and the rig must be directly in line with the wind.

The helicopter

Sometimes called 'sail and sailor 360', this trick is relatively easy in light winds, but becomes increasingly difficult in higher winds.

The trick involves you turning the sail through 360 degrees, while you keep hold of the same side.

Sail head to wind and luff the sail (top left). Pushing the sail clew first through 180 degrees (top right, bottom left), so that it passes through the eye of the wind to windward. (In heavier winds rake the mast more to windward). As the sail passes through the eye of the wind (bottom right) it will pick up speed and you will have to be very quick to stay with it. In the early stages, let go with the sheet hand if necessary.

The pirouette Ken Winner was responsible for developing this spectacular trick. It involves sailing on a close reach, letting go of the rig while spinning a full circle, grabbing the rig and regaining control.

On a port tack first luff the sail slightly to ensure it has the maximum chance of staying stationary. Then spin clockwise. As the turn ends, slow down the spin with one foot just before you grab the boom at the completion of the trick.

Riding the rail is the first real ambition of board sailors who want to do freestyle. This sailor is confident enough to stand with both feet on the rail— the edge of the board.

Below left: *To do the pirouette, first sail on a port tack on a close reach.*
Below centre: *Let go of the boom and spin clockwise.*
Below right: *Grab the boom and sail off.*

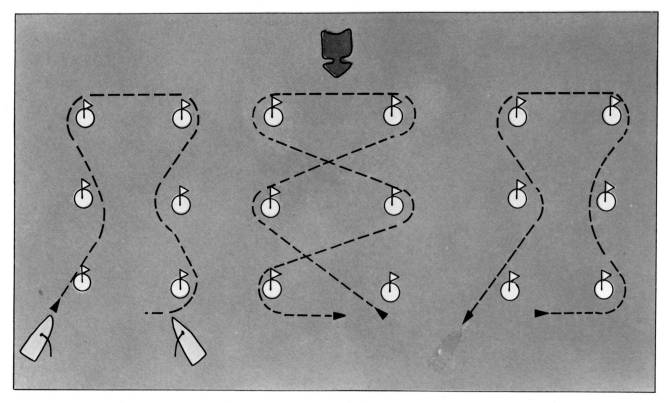

Three laps of a typical slalom course, calling for good technique in tacks and gybes.

Sail board games

Slalom racing

In this event two sail boards match race over the course illustrated on this page. Both sail boards leave simultaneously, firstly tacking up one side of the course, then gybing down the other side. They then alternately tack across and gybe using both sides of the course, finally tacking and gybing on their opponent's original course. Right of way rules apply (port gives way to starboard, see page 59).

Slalom racing pushes a board sailor's ability to tack and gybe at speed to its utmost, and is very good practice for all points of sailing.

Long distance race.

Long distance races vary in length but they can be anything from 18-30km (11-20 miles). They are usually held with the majority of the race sailed on a reach.

A typical course has a one mile beat to windward after a Le Mans style start off a beach. Competitors line their boards up fully rigged on

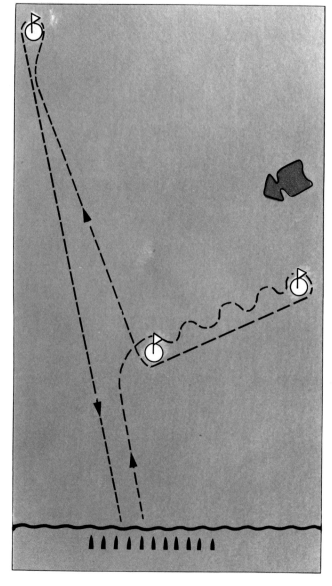

A typical long distance course. A good board sailor will be able to sense and take advantage of wind shifts on the long beat.

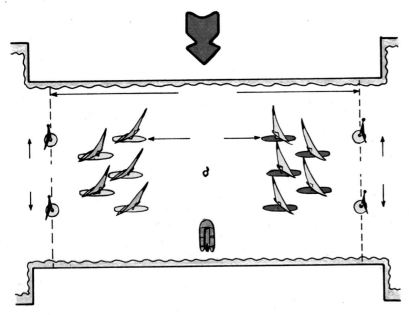

the beach, then sprint to them on the gun from a line about a hundred metres away.

A buoy is moored several hundred metres offshore, this has to be rounded before the first beat is commenced. It is then rounded again after a dead run back from the first beat, before setting out on a very long reach out to sea. This may even be to another town down the coast, an island, shipping buoy or whatever, some 8-10km (five to six miles) away.

Long beats on distance races must be avoided, because the field gets spread over such a wide area that it becomes difficult to provide adequate rescue boat cover.

'Ins and outs' requires racing over both calm water and waves. In this instance the competitors have to gybe around the first mark and tack around the second, repeating this is a given number of times.

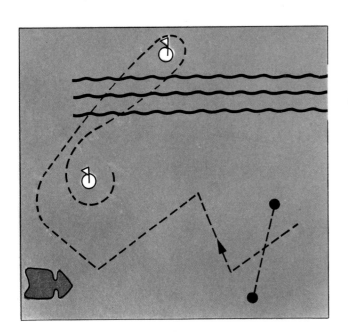

Ideally in buoy ball, the site is chosen so that the wind favours neither side. At the start, the two teams are 20 metres apart and the 'ball' is placed between them.

Buoy – ball

This game is usually only played in very light airs, when it is impossible to race. Two teams of around five players compete against each other in what is a form of sailing rugby.

A 'hoppity toy' or buoy with a handle is used as the ball. The object is to score goals against the opposing teams. Each team has a goal keeper, and possession is gained by touching the other players board or person, whereby he can only drop the buoy and not pass it to another member of his team.

The ball can only be passed from player to player if they are not in contact with one another. The game does have rules, but they tend to be ignored in a heated match, followed by much damage to boards, equipment and players.

Ins and outs

This form of competition can only really be held effectively in an area where a course can be set with flat water and reaching legs in and out through waves and breaking surf.

It involves a short beat to windward, in the flat water, then a reaching course around two buoys laid in waves and surf. 180 degree gybes in surf are not the easiest of manoeuvres, and many thrills and spills occur on the five or six laps of the reaching course.

This game was devised in Hawaii, where there is the additional pleasure of wave jumping and riding during the race.

GLOSSARY

Abeam   At 90 degrees to the board's centre line.
Aft   The stern (back) of the board.
Answering pennant   Red and white flag hoisted when race is postponed.
All-weather sail (4.5m² 48 sq ft)   The sail's area is reduced by having a hollow leech. A normal full-size sail, has a convex leech, with the additional sailcloth held in position by the battens. The all-weather has a concave leech, and is battenless. The entire mast is still used, although there is very little cloth at the head of the sail.
Apparent wind   The wind power resulting from a combination of the true wind and the movement of the sailboard through the water.
Beam reach   Sailing with the wind at 90 degrees to the board.
Bear off   To change direction away from the wind.
Beating   Sailing into the wind on alternate tacks.
Beaufort scale   A scale of wind speed ranging from 0 (calm) to 12 (hurricane).
Blue Peter   The flag hoisted five minutes before a race; a white square on a blue background.
Broad reach   Sailing with the wind slightly behind; between a beam reach and running dead downwind.
Bow scoop (or rocker)   The front of the board where it lifts up.
Centre of effort   An imaginary point at which the different pressures of the windward and leeward side of sail are centered.
Centre of lateral resistance   The point at which the board pivots.
Chine   The edge of the board.
Class flag   The flag hoisted ten minutes before the start of a race.
Close-hauled   Sailing as near as possible into the wind without stalling.
Clew   The eyelet used to secure the sail to the outer edge of the boom.
Daggerboard (centre board)   The removable keel of the board.
Eye of the wind   The direction from which the true wind is blowing.
Foot   The bottom edge of the sail.
Footstrap   Inverted 'U' shaped straps on the board under which the feet are placed (mainly for wave jumping).
General recall   A yellow and blue triangular pennant used to recall the fleet in a race.
Gybe   Changing direction while sailing off the wind.

Head   The top of the sail.
Head to wind   To point the board directly into the wind.
Leech   The trailing edge of the sail.
Leeward   Downwind.
Luff   To bring the board to head to wind, (also the leading edge of the sail).
Luff sleeve   The pocket on the sail into which the mast is pushed.
Marginal sail (4.5-4.8m² 48-50 sq ft)   It is cut with a straight leech from about 30cm (1 ft) down the mast and has a very high clew. This prevents the boom dragging in the water when riding down the front of large waves. Using this sail should only be considered by an experienced sailor.
Mast inhaul   Rope which attaches front of boom to mast.
Mast leash   Safety line preventing rig and board from completely separating.
Plane   The tendency of the daggerboard to lift out of the water at speed.
Port   The left side of the board when looking forward.
Pumping   The action of pulling the sail towards you to gain power (especially when running downwind).
Rake   To tilt the mast.
Running (dead before the wind)   Sailing with the wind directly behind.
Sail outhaul   Rope which attaches the clew of the sail to the rear of the boom.
Sheet in   To bring the sail closer to the body.
Skeg   The small fin at the rear of the board.
Starboard   The right of the board when looking forward.
Storm sail (3.5m² 37 sq ft)   The smallest sail available is designed to be used by the average size person in winds over force six. The sail area is reduced down the leech, leaving a length of mast unused at the head.
Tack   The eyelet at the bottom of a sail.
Tacking   To sail upwind on alternate courses.
True wind   The wind that is blowing at the time.
Upwind   Movement against the direction of the wind.
Universal joint   The linkage at the foot of the mast that allows the mast to be tilted in any direction.
Windward   The direction from which the wind is coming.
Wishbone   The boom onto which the board sailor holds.

INDEX